Ice Cream!

Delicious ice creams for all occasions

Pippa Cuthbert &
Lindsay Cameron Wilson

Good Books

Intercourse, PA 17534
800/762-7171
www.goodbks.com

Dedication
For Luke and Sophie

First published in North America by
Good Books
Intercourse, PA 17534
800/762 - 7171
www.goodbks.com

ICE CREAM!
Good Books, Intercourse, PA 17534
International Standard Book Number: 1-56148-476-8
(paperback edition)
International Standard Book Number: 1-56148-477-6
(comb-bound paperback edition)

Library of Congress Catalog Card Number: 2004024549

   Library of Congress Cataloging-in-Publication Data

Cuthbert, Pippa.
    Ice Cream! : delicious ice creams for all occasions /
Pippa Cuthbert and Lindsay Cameron Wilson.
           p. cm.
Includes bibliographical references and index.
    ISBN 1-56148-476-8 (pbk.) -- ISBN 1-56148-477-6
(comb) 1. Ice cream, ices, etc. I. Wilson, Lindsay
Cameron. II. Title.
    TX795.C88 2005
    641.8'62--dc22

                    2004024549

Senior Editor: Clare Hubbard
Editor: Anna Bennett
Design: Paul Wright
Photography: Stuart West
Food styling: Pippa Cuthbert and Lindsay Cameron Wilson
Production: Ben Byram-Wigfield
Editorial Direction: Rosemary Wilkinson

Reproduction by Pica Digital PTE Ltd, Singapore
Printed and bound by C & C Offset Printing, China

Acknowledgments
Many thanks to Camilla Schneideman at Divertimenti
(www.divertimenti.co.uk) and Lindy Wiffen at Ceramica Blue
(www.ceramicablue.co.uk) for their friendship and gorgeous
props. Thanks also to our discerning testers, who sacrificed
their waistlines for our book.

Note
Due to the slight risk of salmonella, recipes containing raw
eggs should not be served to children, to the ill or elderly or
to pregnant women.

Contents

Introduction

Let's face it. Serving food to friends is at least partly about showing off. Everyone needs a party trick, and personal, edible creations are on top of the crowd-pleasing list. It's human nature.

The purpose of this book is to make ice cream everyone's party trick. It's a simple, make-ahead treat that involves no sweating in the kitchen and will always impress. Most people think of homemade ice cream as being too difficult to tackle, but we have a secret: making ice cream is easy. Throughout the book we expose this truth through our well-tested recipes. Whether it's an ice cream, sorbet, parfait, semifreddo or granita, if you use the best ingredients you can find and if you adhere to our guidelines, all will be well.

Of course, there will always be people in this world who insist on making the simple complicated. Heston Blumenthal, an English three-starred Michelin chef and molecular gastronomist, prefers to tease the palate by serving bacon and egg ice cream in a pot of liquid nitrogen. Or how about Hokkaido, a Japanese ice cream manufacturer that has captured the essence of corn, sweet potato or crab in its ice creams. Never fear. Our innovative flavor combinations will titillate, not shock, the palate, and our methods are traditional. We explore classic flavors such as vanilla, chocolate and fresh strawberry. For the more adventurous, there is Cinnamon and Mascarpone Ice Cream, Lavender Frozen Yogurt or Marmalade Parfait. Old favorites are revisited but given an innovative twist, while fruit sorbet reaches new heights with interesting flavor combinations such as blackberries and Cabernet Sauvignon.

Each recipe is made from luxurious ingredients – from creamy, organic dairy products and rich, dark chocolate to ripe, seasonal fruits. Once the shopping is complete, all that is required is either an ice cream maker or an electric whisk, patience while freezing and a desire for fame.

There is always a place in our lives for ice cream, regardless of the weather, the temperature, the event or the time of year. The recipes in this book are created for all these moments – from dinner parties to children's parties, afternoons in the garden to rainy days under the quilt. Pippa and I got hooked on making ice cream in London, a city better known for rainy winters than long, scorching summer days. Perhaps it's because ice creams soothe, impress or simply fulfill a culinary urge, regardless of the climate in which you find yourself. After all, the kings of ice cream, Ben and Jerry, made their fortune selling ice cream in the wintry city of Burlington, Vermont. They argued that when it's cold outside we have a desire to fill our bodies with cold food in order to balance our body temperature. Maybe they have a point. Regardless of their theories, their pint-size ice cream tubs are now permanent fixtures in freezers around the world. However, opening a tub of store-bought ice cream, no matter how tasty, just doesn't cut it as a party trick. So let's hear it for real ice cream. Discover new ingredients and enter fearlessly into the simple yet sensational world of ice cream making.

Chemistry of ice cream

To make successful ice cream, it helps if you understand the chemistry of how and why each ingredient is important. A little knowledge will give you the freedom to play with recipes, and the confidence to predict the end result. Whether you prefer a calorific and creamy semifreddo or a rich gelato, the result is up to you. As time goes by and your ice cream repertoire increases, you'll become an ice cream expert. Learning is all part of the journey.

How ice cream is made

Ice cream is a foam that is stabilized by freezing much of the liquid. In its frozen state, ice cream is made up of some liquids containing dissolved salts, sugars, suspended milk proteins and milk fats. Two important aspects of the freezing process that also affect the final texture of your ice cream are the number and size of ice crystals and the amount of air incorporated during freezing.

Milk and cream

It is the globules of milk fat present in milk and cream that give ice cream its rich, creamy and smooth texture. Essentially, the greater the percentage of milk fats, the creamier the end product will be. However, to avoid a dense end product, it is important to ensure that you have a proportion of the milk fats in their homogenized state. It is milk, not cream, that contains homogenized fats. Your ice cream will incorporate air more readily with more homogenized fats and protein present. It will produce a lighter and less calorific end product.

An ice cream with more cream and less milk will be denser and creamier. Unless you prefer a very dense ice cream, we suggest that you always use a combination of milk and cream. The amount and ratio you use will depend on your individual taste.

Sugars and sweeteners

Ice cream requires the inclusion of some sort of sweetener, whether sugar, honey or maple syrup (see page 15). Sugars or sweeteners lower the freezing point of ice cream. During the initial phase of ice cream making, the sugars are dissolved by beating or by heat when a syrup or custard is made. Once cooled, the dissolved sugar gets in the way of the water molecules that must bond together to form ice crystals, lowering the freezing point of the solution. It is the presence of sugar that means the liquid phase of ice cream will never freeze completely. It is also important to understand that as your ice cream freezes, the sweetness of the sugar also decreases. You may find your sugar syrup too sweet or your custard too rich, but once the mixture has been frozen, you will notice that the sweetness is reduced.

Eggs

Eggs help to improve the texture of your ice cream by acting as an emulsifying agent, suspending the milk fat globules. Eggs will also improve the foaming ability of your ice cream, allowing more air to be incorporated. Both these factors result in a creamier, richer end product. Most commercial ice creams are egg-free, because ice cream manufacturers add emulsifying agents to their products.

Ice crystals

It is the number and size of ice crystals that will influence the texture of your ice cream. Larger ice crystals result in a coarser texture, and finer crystals will give you a more desirable creamy texture. It is the speed at which the ice cream mixture cools that determines how large the resulting crystals will be. Rapid freezing ensures the simultaneous production of small crystals that are evenly distributed and prevents crystals clumping together. Ideally, this rapid freezing requires the use of an ice cream maker. When an ice cream maker is not available, and freezing your ice cream mixture in the freezer is the only option, it is important to stir the mixture frequently during the freezing process to try and break down the crystal clumps before they freeze solid (see page 17, Still freezing method). Make sure you store your ice cream correctly (see page 21), as any moisture that settles on the surface of the ice cream will form large ice crystals.

Air particles

The amount of air incorporated during the freezing process is the invisible but essential ingredient that prevents your ice cream from freezing into a solid block. As the ice cream maker churns, it traps air particles, causing the ice cream to increase in volume. Most commercial ice cream machines pump considerable amounts of compressed air into the ice cream at the end of freezing. Most commercial ice creams contain 50 percent air, which is the legal maximum. Ice creams made at home will incorporate much smaller amounts of air, producing a higher-quality product.

Extras but not essentials
Flavorings
The addition of flavorings such as vanilla, cinnamon and rosewater will have little effect on the final texture of your ice cream. It is the addition of ingredients such as fruit and chocolate that will influence the texture more significantly. Essentially, ingredients with a high moisture or water content will have the most effect and should be compensated for. As a general rule, fruit contains a high proportion of water and natural sugars. The extra water will dilute the ice cream mixture and change the final texture. When adding fruit, it is important to increase the amount of fat globules to make up for this; the mixture should have a proportionately higher cream content than milk. If you are adding fruits with high sugar content, such as bananas, the amount of added sugar should be decreased. Fruits with a low sugar content, such as raspberries, require additional sugar.

Alcohol
Alcohol, like sugar, lowers the point of freezing. When you add alcohol to your ice cream mixture, it will always take longer to freeze. If you add too much alcohol to your mixture, it will not freeze at all. Don't go adding an extra splash for flavor, because you'll only end up with unsuccessful results.

This is the one time we ask you to stick to the recipe. You need only enough alcohol to just be able to taste it!

Chocolate chunks, cookies and candy
When you are adding larger chunks to your ice cream, always add these toward the end of freezing, or they will sink to the bottom. Once the ice cream has finished churning, stir the chunks into the mixture to prevent clogging up the maker. If you are making the ice cream without using an ice cream maker, add the chunks after the third or fourth stirring.

Important ingredients

VANILLA
Vanilla bean
The vanilla bean, from a climbing orchid plant native to Central America, will indisputably give your ice cream the best vanilla flavor. Good-quality beans should be soft, deep brown in color with a warm and fragrant aroma and flavor. For tips on how best to remove the seeds from a vanilla bean, see page 18.

Vanilla extract
When time and money are limited, your next best alternative to a bean is vanilla "extract" – the "pure" and "natural" distilled extract from the bean. The word "extract" ensures that the product is derived from the vanilla bean. Avoid any imitation or synthetic vanilla "essences." Essences are used in most cheap ice creams and leave a lingering artificial aftertaste. Vanilla "essence" is often made from just one component of vanilla "extract" – vanillin. It is vanillin, in combination with substances such as gums, resins and oils, that makes the "extract."

Check the bottle for words such as "extract," "pure" or "natural" and avoid anything labeled "essence," "synthetic" or "imitation."

Pure vanilla paste
Pure vanilla paste is another convenient and high-quality replacement for vanilla beans in any recipe, especially in ice cream. The paste still contains the vanilla bean seeds and adds a speckled appearance to foods. You should be able to find vanilla paste at any quality supermarket or delicatessen.

1 Tbsp pure vanilla paste = 1 vanilla bean or 1 Tbsp vanilla extract

CHOCOLATE

Chocolate is one of life's great indulgences, and ice cream is another. Combine the two and you have the ultimate dessert: chocolate ice cream is the world's second most popular ice cream flavor after vanilla. Chocolate is obtained from the cocoa bean, which has been roasted, cracked and then husked to expose the nibs. The nibs are then ground with water to produce the cocoa liquor or mass. This cocoa mass can then be further reduced to produce cocoa butter and cocoa powder. It is the percentage of cocoa mass or cocoa solids in chocolate that gives it its taste.

Bittersweet and semisweet chocolate

Bittersweet chocolate can generally contain anything up to 95 percent cocoa solids with no added sugar. This chocolate is extremely bitter, glossy, smooth and almost red in color. It melts easily and breaks off cleanly. Semisweet chocolate has the addition of sugar and a lower percentage of cocoa solids, usually about 50–70 percent.

We recommend the use of chocolate with at least 60 percent cocoa solids.

Milk chocolate

Milk chocolate has milk solids and sugar added to it, giving it a lower percentage of cocoa solids – usually about 10–30 percent. It is sweeter and creamier in texture than plain chocolate, with a less intense taste. Children often prefer this less bitter alternative, particularly in ice cream.

White chocolate

Technically, white chocolate is not chocolate at all. It contains only cocoa butter, milk solids and sugar, but no cocoa solids. Vanilla flavoring is often added, so check for terms such as "natural" or "pure" on the label, which will give you a clue as to its quality. White chocolate is not readily interchangeable with other chocolate. It must be treated more delicately, because it has a tendency to seize. To "seize" means to stiffen and will happen when chocolate comes into contact with steam. Seized chocolate cannot be re-melted. You must start again if this happens.

Unsweetened cocoa

Cocoa is a by-product of chocolate. It is produced, along with cocoa butter, when the cocoa solids or cocoa liquor are pressed during the manufacture of chocolate. Cocoa is used in its dried, powdered form and has no added sugar. It has a final fat content of between 10–35 percent.

Pure chocolate extract

Chocolate extract is becoming more widely available. It is a low-fat chocolate alternative, particularly useful in ice cream making. It is very important to check the packaging to ensure the product is "natural" and "pure" – if no description is given, don't buy the product, because it is likely to be an imitation.

EGGS

We have used large eggs, average weight 2¼–2½oz (65–70g), throughout. If you have leftover egg whites, bag them and freeze them, clearly marking the date and number of whites. Use them within 4 months. Allow the whites to thaw overnight in the refrigerator or under hot running water and use immediately once defrosted. Frozen whites should only be used for recipes in which the white is thoroughly cooked – not in ice cream!

MILK

In all recipes, unless otherwise specified, we have used whole milk, which has a milk fat percentage of 4 percent. We would advise against the use of UHT (ultra heat treated), or long life milk, because of its adverse effects on the taste and consistency of your ice cream. We have used many by-products of milk such as yogurt (see page 14), sour cream, crème fraîche and cream cheese, and also other types of milk such as condensed milk and soy milk.

CREAM

Cream is a form of milk in which the fat globules have been concentrated by reducing the water content using a centrifugal method.

For simplicity's sake, we have tried to use only one cream type to keep shopping easy and the refrigerator uncluttered. Heavy cream (48 percent fat content) is our standard.

The three grades of cream marketed today are usually categorized as;
Light (pouring) cream – approx.
   20% milk fat
Whipping cream – approx.
   36–40% milk fat
Heavy cream – approx. 48% milk fat
The higher the fat content, the thicker, smoother and richer the taste will be and the more stable the product during cooking.

Due to the higher fat content of heavy cream, we have used it in combination with milk in almost all our recipes. This reduces the overall fat content and introduces those essential homogenized fats.

YOGURT

Yogurt is fermented and coagulated milk. It is the result of milk sugars (lactose) being converted to lactic acid. In all recipes where yogurt is used, you will find we have opted for full-fat creamy Greek yogurt, which has a fat content of approximately 10 percent. If you use yogurt with a lower fat content than this, there is a chance of it separating in the ice cream mixture and producing an icy layer.

FRUIT

This is probably the most important group of ingredients to mention, because it has the most variables. Taste, texture, water content, sweetness and color can all vary, depending on how fresh your chosen fruit is and whether it is in season.

All fruits contain a high proportion of water and some sugar, but it is important to understand that all fruits are different. The sugar content of a banana, for example, is much greater than the sugar content of a raspberry, and an apple contains less water per weight than a watermelon. The amount of sugar and water added to each recipe is calculated in order to account for the fruit's natural content, but this will vary, depending on the season. When making ice cream, it is always advisable to choose fruit that is in season and of the highest quality if you want to produce a premium end product with good flavor, color and texture. Organic fruit is our preferred

choice when available, because its flavor is often more intense and the skins free of sprays and pesticides.

WATER

Water from the faucet is quite variable in composition, depending on its ultimate source and treatment. In London, for example, the water contains large amounts of calcium and magnesium ions, resulting in so-called hard water, which can affect the color and texture of some foods. For this reason, we recommend always using filtered or bottled still water. Basically, if you prefer not to drink the water from your faucet, then don't make ices with it.

Rosewater

Rosewater is made from the distillation of rose petals and is commonly used in the Middle East and India to flavor both sweet and savory dishes. This should be available at your local supermarket and can usually be found in the baking section.

Orange flower water

Orange flower water is made from the distillation of orange blossoms. It should be available in the baking section of your local supermarket.

SUGAR AND SWEETENERS

Extra-fine sugar

Extra-fine sugar is used in all the recipes unless otherwise specified. The smaller crystals or finer grains allow extra-fine sugar to incorporate more air than other sugars, which makes it perfect for creating a light and creamy ice cream. The finer grains also dissolve faster, which is ideal if you are making syrup and custard ice cream bases.

Vanilla sugar

Store-bought vanilla sugar is usually made by adding vanilla extract to extra-fine sugar. It is simple, and certainly much cheaper, to make your own: just add a vanilla bean to an airtight jar filled with extra-fine sugar and allow the flavor and aroma to infuse for at least a week. You will then have a wonderful, vanilla-fragranced sugar.

Brown sugar

When a richer, caramel flavor is desired, we have used a variety of brown sugars: soft brown sugar (light or dark), raw brown sugar (larger crystals), molasses sugar or muscovado (light or dark) sugars. Brown sugar is white sugar with molasses added to it.

Confectioner's sugar

Confectioner's sugar is a powdery, brilliant white sugar that dissolves instantly when mixed with liquid.

Corn syrup

Honeylike in texture, this is a by-product of the sugar-refining process. Corn syrup adds distinctive flavor and color to ice cream.

Maple syrup

Watch for maple syrup that has a maple leaf on the label: this guarantees the authenticity of the product and its origin. Avoid products labeled "maple-flavored" if you can. Maple syrup is the boiled-down sap of certain kinds of maple tree native to Canada and America. It gives a sweetness and a distinctive flavor.

Honey

The flavor and aroma of honey depend on the flowers from which the nectar has been obtained. Single-flower honeys are usually the best. The general rule is that the darker the honey, the stronger the flavor, so choose a honey based on how dominant you want the flavor to be.

Practical tips

Equipment

The following pieces of equipment will make ices a whole lot easier:

- Ice cream maker, at least 2–3 pt (1.5-L) capacity
- Heavy-bottomed saucepans
- Double boiler, or a stainless steel bowl that fits above a saucepan
- Measuring cups and spoons
- Sugar thermometer
- Wire mesh sieve and cheesecloth
- Blender
- Grater or rasp
- Wire whisks and wooden spoons
- Waxed paper, baking parchment, plastic wrap or foil
- Freezer containers
- Ice cream scoops
- Popsicle molds

Ice cream makers

You don't need an ice cream maker to make great ice cream, but, as with so many things, appliances make the job much easier. There are three basic styles of machines on the market, all ranging in function, form and cost.

If a little nostalgia and bigger biceps are what you're after, then an old-fashioned manual machine is for you. Ice cream, frozen yogurts and sorbets are made as you sit, churn and reminisce. Two buckets make the process possible – the inner bucket holds the ice cream, while the outer bucket holds the ice and salt (salt lowers the temperature of the ice). The benefit? Churning your own ice cream gives you complete control over the final product.

At the opposite end of the spectrum is a smaller version of professional ice cream makers with a self-contained freezer unit and a powerful motor. Simply turn on the machine, wait a few minutes, pour in the mix and, in less than an hour, your creation is ready. The benefits? The ability spontaneously to produce fantastic ice cream in under an hour. The downfall? It's as expensive as it is large. It's either the microwave or the ice cream maker, I'm afraid; one will have to go.

The latest, most affordable option is an electric ice cream maker with a bucket that must be prefrozen. All of the recipes in this book were tested on this style of machine. Remove the prefrozen bucket from the freezer, attach it to the motor and pour your mix through the spout on top; your ice cream, sorbet or frozen yogurt will be ready in around 20 minutes. The benefits? It's compact, quick and affordable. The downfall? The bucket must be prefrozen, which makes spontaneous ice cream making difficult. But, if there's enough room in your freezer, keep the bucket in there all the time for those "must have ice cream" moments.

Still freezing method

If you do not own an ice cream maker, you can still make every ice cream in this book by using the still freezing method. To freeze your ice cream mixture successfully, it is important to ensure you set your freezer temperature to 0°F (-18°C) or, alternatively, to use the fast-freeze option if you have it. When your ice cream mixture is made, transfer it to a suitable freezer container, cover it and place it in the coldest part of the freezer. Leave for about 1–1½ hours, or until the sides and base are just frozen and the middle is a soft slush. Remove from the freezer and beat, using an electric whisk or food processor, until the ice crystals are uniform. It is important to work quickly to prevent the ice crystals from melting. Cover the mixture and quickly return to the freezer. Repeat this process two more times, at 1–1½-hour intervals. If you are adding large chunks, such as chocolate, broken cookies or candy, add them after the third or fourth beating. After the final beating, allow the ice cream to freeze for at least 2 hours, or preferably overnight before serving.

It is not necessary to beat a semifreddo while still freezing – just cover the surface and freeze for at least 6 hours.

Handy hints and techniques

To beat egg whites…
Make sure that the bowl and beater are immaculately clean and dry before separating your eggs, because any trace of fat can prevent the egg white from beating successfully. A quick rub of the bowl with half a lemon will take away any greasy residue. Carefully separate the egg yolks from the whites; there should be no traces of yolk in the whites, because this may also prevent beating. Make sure your eggs are at room temperature; they

will beat more quickly and to a greater volume than egg whites taken straight from the refrigerator. Be careful not to overbeat your whites, or they will become dry and will not easily blend or fold with other ingredients.

Occasionally, our recipes call for lightly beaten egg whites; to do this, just whisk the whites several times using a fork. They should not become foamy, but you should achieve a slightly more free-pouring consistency. Soft peaks are when the peaked foam falls back on itself when the whisk is removed. Stiff peaks hold their peaked shape when the whisk is removed.

To fold together ingredients…
Always use a large, clean metal spoon when folding ingredients. Gently pull the spoon through the center of the ingredients, from the back of the bowl to the front, in a cutting motion. Repeat this motion several times until the ingredients are just combined. The idea of folding is to retain as much air in the mixture as possible; do not beat the mixture or the air bubbles will collapse and your mixture will sink, resulting in a less creamy ice cream.

To scrape a vanilla bean…
Split the vanilla bean lengthwise using a small, sharp knife. Take one half and place it on a flat surface with the seeds facing up. Using the back of the blade, run the knife from one end of the bean to the other, moving it away from your body, adding enough pressure to collect all the seeds as you go. Repeat this with the second half. The seeds will all gather together in a clump, but once added to your mixture they will separate and disperse evenly throughout the ice cream, producing a speckled effect.

To whip cream…

Make sure that your cream is well chilled before whipping, and that your beaters and bowl are also cool (not straight from the dishwasher!). This is especially important in summer, when the weather is warmer. The action of whipping will inevitably warm up the cream, so the cooler it is to start, the longer you have to incorporate air. The whipping action introduces air bubbles into the liquid that are then stabilized by the proteins contained in the liquid and given extra reinforcement by the fat globules present. Cream can be whipped to several stages; soft and stiff peaks are the most commonly used stages in our recipes. Soft peaks are when the peaked cream falls back on itself when the beaters are removed. Stiff peaks hold their peaked shape when the beaters are removed.

To make a custard…

Many of the recipes specify beating the mixture in a heatproof bowl over a saucepan of simmering water. The ideal is a medium-size bowl with low, curved edges – one you can still reach into when it is placed on top of a saucepan – and its base should firmly fit into the top of your saucepan and feel secure. Pyrex, stainless steel or any other heatproof material will be suitable. The water should be simmering, or at a constant just-below-boiling point where very small bubbles form. It is important to ensure that the water level never touches the base of the bowl. Beating or stirring should always be constant; make sure that you move the beater or spoon evenly around the whole bowl, incorporating all of the ingredients. When making a custard base for your ice cream, the mixture should be heated until it is thick enough to coat the back of a wooden spoon. This means your mixture should be smooth and silky and just thick enough to hold a viscous coating over the back of a spoon when the spoon is removed from the mixture. Do not overheat the mixture, or the custard will begin to separate or split. If this happens, the custard can be rescued by placing the bowl over a bowl of ice cubes and whisking vigorously.

To melt chocolate…

The most reliable method of melting chocolate is in a heatproof bowl over a saucepan of simmering water. Make sure that the bowl firmly fits the saucepan and does not touch the water. Break the chocolate into pieces before adding it to the bowl and stir constantly while the chocolate melts, allowing about 4–6 minutes. Chocolate can also be melted in a microwave oven. Microwave on medium for 1 minute, then stir. Repeat the process until all the chocolate has melted.

Avoid overheating or allowing water or steam to come in contact with the chocolate, as it may "seize" or stiffen. If this happens, you will have to start over again; there is no going back.

To zest citrus fruits...

It is important when zesting citrus fruits not to remove too much of the bitter white pith. It is best to use a sharp potato peeler that will remove just the outer layer of zest into long strips – this is ideal for infusing syrups and sorbets. Alternatively, use a fine grater and grate the zest until the white is just visible, but no further.

To toast nuts...

Toasting nuts is one of the simplest things to do, yet one of the easiest things to forget; so make sure you set a timer. There is nothing worse than burned nuts and having to start again. Spread the whole nuts evenly, in a single layer, in a shallow baking sheet. Bake in a preheated oven, 350°F (180°C), for 10–12 minutes or until the nuts are golden brown. If toasting chopped nuts, keep an even closer eye on them, because they won't take as long to brown – about 5–6 minutes depending on their size.

To caramelize condensed milk...

Be extremely careful when caramelizing condensed milk, and do not allow children to do this. Place the can in a large saucepan of near-boiling water that comes to just below the top of the can. (As the water evaporates, keep topping it up to this level.) Leave the water on a very gentle boil for 2 hours, then remove the can from the water. Allow the now caramelized condensed milk to cool before opening the can.

To crystallize petals...

Choose your favorite edible flowers or petals (e.g. roses, violets or geraniums) and remove any visible dirt from them. Make sure the flowers or petals are dry before you start. In a small bowl, combine one large egg white (room temperature) and a few drops of water and beat lightly with a fork. Have about 1 cup (190g) extra-fine sugar ready in a shallow dish with a fine sieve. Holding a flower or petal in one hand, dip a clean, small paint-brush (reserved for food use only) into the egg white with the other hand and gently paint the flower or petal. Holding the flower over the sugar dish, sift a light coating of sugar evenly over both sides. Place the flower or petal on baking parchment to dry, and continue with the rest. You can leave the flowers to dry for 12–36 hours in a relatively moisture-free area. Alternatively, place the crystallized flowers or petals in an oven set at 225°F (110°C) with the door ajar for 3–4 hours. Store in airtight containers for up to 1 year.

To toast coconut...

Place the coconut in a thin layer on a baking sheet. Bake in a preheated oven, 325°F (160°C), for 10–15 minutes, or until the coconut is golden brown, stirring occasionally. Alternatively, place the coconut in a shallow, microwave-safe dish and microwave on high for 1 minute, then stir. Repeat until the coconut is golden brown.

To make a sugar syrup...

Put equal measures of extra-fine sugar and water in a heavy-based saucepan. Place over gentle heat until the sugar has dissolved, without boiling the mixture. Increase the heat and bring to a boil. Boil the syrup for a further 5 minutes. Remove from the heat and cool completely before using.

To clean a saucepan used to make caramel...

The saucepan will benefit from a little post-caramel simmer. Fill it with water and a dash of vinegar or lemon juice and put it back on the heat. Simmer until the sugar dissolves and washes away easily.

To store ice cream properly...

Always cover the surface of your ice cream directly with baking parchment or foil. This prevents large ice crystals from forming on the surface. It will also prevent odors from other foodstuffs in the freezer contaminating your ice cream. We recommend that you eat your ice cream within 2–3 weeks of making it – unlike bought ice creams, homemade ice creams contain no preservatives.

To scoop ice cream...

Whether it's a curl, a ball or a quenelle you're after, there are many ways to scoop ice cream. Whatever you use to scoop with, you should always dip it in a bowl of hot water between each scoop to stop the ice cream from sticking. It is also important to have your ice cream at a scoopable texture. For each recipe, we have given guidelines on when to remove the ice cream from the freezer if softening time is required.

- To create a curl of ice cream, use a classic oval scoop with a beaked tip and drag this along the ice cream – great with desserts.
- Use a rounded mechanical scoop to create a perfect ball – ideal for sundaes, sodas and cones.
- Create a chef-style quenelle scoop by using two tablespoons. Turn the ice cream repeatedly between the two spoons until it forms an oval.

In recipe ingredients list:
Tbsp = tablespoon
tsp = teaspoon
L = liter

Quantities given for how much the recipe makes are approximate.

Definition of ices

Take two parts hydrogen and one part oxygen. Leave below freezing and there you have it – ice. This recipe has occurred naturally on earth ever since the very first frost. Yet how did it make the gastronomic leap into the world of frozen dessert?

Well, it all started in the cold regions of ancient China, where food was commonly left outdoors in the snow to freeze. The Chinese introduced this method of preservation to the Arabs. They in turn made *sharbahs*, drinks of sweetened fruit juices or flower-infused syrups poured over ice or snow. It was the Turks, in particular, who introduced sweetened ice to the Italians, who introduced it to the rest of Europe. Today, myriad ices are available throughout the world, some made from fruit syrups, others with the addition of cream, chocolate, nuts or herbs. Their names vary from sorbets to granitas, parfaits to ice creams, but one thing remains the same: without ice, they wouldn't exist. For linguistic ease, throughout the book we will refer to the various types of ice creams and sorbets as "ices."

Ice cream
Ice cream is the most famous of foods made with dairy products. It is thought that the first ice cream was made in Italy and then France in the seventeenth century, when cream was added to *sorbetti*, or sorbets. By the end of the eighteenth century, ice cream recipes were featured in English language cook books. Americans shared the English taste for ice cream and adopted the dish as their own. Today, it is the world's most popular dessert.

Ice cream can generally be divided into two categories: those made with a cooked egg custard base and those made with just sweetened cream. European ice creams are generally based on the former method, while American-style ice creams follow the latter. Both methods include the addition of a flavoring ingredient, such as vanilla or chocolate, and often other ingredients, such as chocolate chunks, fruit or nuts, added before or during the freezing process.

Sorbet and sherbet
The provenance of the above is most likely the French and English attempts at the Arab word *sharbah*, a sweetened fruit juice or flower-infused syrup poured over ice or snow. Today, the *sharbah* has evolved into a fruit-based ice dessert (sorbet), made by churning sweetened fruit juices in an ice cream maker. The motion of

the dasher keeps the crystals from growing too large, creating very fine ice crystals. Sorbets can be made without an ice cream maker by frequently stirring the mixture during the freezing process.

Sherbet generally describes a sorbet that has the addition of milk or cream.

Fruit granita
A fruit granita is a sorbet of sorts, but it has a chunkier, coarser texture. Granitas are made by chopping the mixture by hand rather than churning it in an ice cream maker. This method naturally creates larger, more textured crystals. Chopping can be done with stainless steel pastry scrapers, a metal spatula, two knives or, at a pinch, a fork. Granitas are best served within two days.

Semifreddo
This means "half cold" in Italian. In the culinary sense, it refers to any partially frozen dessert, from cake to ice cream, fruit or custard.

Frozen yogurt
Several ice creams in this book include yogurt as the primary dairy ingredient. Yogurt cuts down on fat content, while its slightly sour taste balances other sweet ingredients.

Tortoni
A rich dessert that traditionally consists of chilled whipped cream flavored with spirits and topped with a combination of chopped nuts or cookie crumbs. We've taken culinary liberties with our version of a tortoni, adding beaten egg whites, toasted coconut and chopped chocolate.

Parfait
Parfait is the French word for "perfect" – what better way to describe ice cream layered with flavored syrup and topped with whipped cream, nuts and a cherry served in its very own tall, narrow "parfait" glass? In France, however, a parfait is made by combining custard cream, a flavored syrup mixed with egg yolks or a fruit purée and whipped cream. Traditionally, the mixture is then frozen in a cylindrical parfait mold. Feel free to break away from the traditional parfait mold, because whatever you have on hand will be – parfait.

Kulfi
Kulfi is India's traditional ice cream. It is made by boiling milk and reducing its volume before adding flavorings such as pistachios or rosewater. It has a harder texture than most Western ice creams and is usually frozen in a conically shaped mold.

Mother ices

In a classic French kitchen, basic sauces are always on hand. They are called mother sauces, for they give birth to myriad others that distinctly characterize French cookery. A family tree can be constructed, mother sauces being the trunk, with the branches as the offspring.

Any well-versed ice cream gastronome will tell you that mother ices also exist. They are the foundations of the ice cream world; although they are delicious on their own, they provide the groundwork for many other ices and ice cream-based desserts. From Vanilla ice cream comes Strawberry ice cream, from Coffee ice cream comes Ice cream affogato, from Dark chocolate ice cream comes Chocolate and hazelnut swirl. And the best offspring of all? The sundae: a melange of all or any of the mother ices, bathed in hot fudge sauce, coated in whipped cream and crowned with a cherry.

Never prune your ice cream tree – experiment with ingredients and flavor combinations, so it will continue to blossom and grow, forever.

the foundations

Vanilla ice cream

Creamy

Universally the world's most popular ice cream! It is paramount that all your ingredients are "pure" and "natural" – any artificial vanilla flavoring will only leave you disappointed.

Makes 3¼ cups (800ml)

1¼ cups (300ml) **whole milk**
1 **vanilla bean**
4 **large egg yolks**
½ cup (100g) **vanilla sugar**
1¼ cups (300ml) **heavy cream**

Put the milk and the vanilla bean, split in half lengthwise, in a medium saucepan and heat gently to near-boiling point. Remove the saucepan from the heat and allow the vanilla to infuse for 15 minutes.

In a separate, heatproof bowl, beat the egg yolks and sugar, using an electric whisk, until thick and pale. Remove the vanilla bean from the milk, scraping out the seeds, and gradually beat the milk into the egg mixture.

Place the bowl over a saucepan of simmering water and continue stirring until the mixture is thick enough to coat the back of a wooden spoon. Remove the bowl from the heat and cover the surface directly with plastic wrap or waxed paper to prevent a skin from forming. Allow the custard to cool completely.

Once cool, stir in the cream and churn in an ice cream maker, according to the manufacturer's instructions. Serve immediately or transfer to a freezer container, cover the surface directly with waxed paper or foil and put in the freezer.

Vanilla ice cream

Strawberry ice cream

Strawberry ice cream

Fragrant

Strawberry is the world's third most popular ice cream flavor, after vanilla and chocolate. This one certainly hits the spot. It's full of fruity strawberry flavor unlike the artificially flavored strawberry ice cream usually found at the supermarket.

Makes 3¼ cups (800ml)

1¼ cups (350g) **strawberries** hulled
1¼ cups (300ml) **whole milk**
4 **large egg yolks**
¾ cup (150g) **extra-fine sugar**
⅔ cup (150ml) **heavy cream**

Put the strawberries in a food processor or blender and blend to a purée. Pass the strawberry purée through a fine sieve or cheesecloth to remove the seeds. Discard the seeds and set the purée aside in the refrigerator.

Pour the milk into a medium saucepan and heat to near-boiling point. While the milk is heating, beat the egg yolks and sugar in a heatproof bowl, using an electric whisk, until thick and pale. Place over a saucepan of simmering water and stir in the warm milk. Stir occasionally until the mixture is thick enough to coat the back of a wooden spoon. Remove from the heat, cover and allow to cool completely.

Add the cream and strawberry purée to the cooled custard. Churn in an ice cream maker, according to the manufacturer's instructions. Serve immediately or transfer to a freezer container, cover the surface directly with waxed paper or foil and put in the freezer.

Milk chocolate ice cream

Indulgent

There are two kinds of chocolate lovers in this world – those who love milk chocolate and those who prefer dark. For the former, here is our milk chocolate version. It has a creamy texture with just the right amount of chocolate.

Makes 2½ cups (600ml)

1 cup (250ml) **whole milk**
2 **large egg yolks**
¼ cup (50g) **extra-fine sugar**
3½oz (100g) **good-quality milk chocolate**
   broken into pieces
1¾oz (50g) **bittersweet chocolate (70% cocoa solids)**
   broken into pieces
⅔ cup (150ml) **heavy cream**

Place the milk in a medium saucepan and heat gently to near-boiling point. Beat the egg yolks and sugar in a heatproof bowl, using an electric whisk, until thick and pale. Gradually beat the milk into the egg mixture.

Place the bowl over a saucepan of simmering water and continue stirring until the mixture is thick enough to coat the back of a wooden spoon. Remove the bowl from the heat and stir in the chocolate pieces, stirring until smooth. Cover the surface directly with plastic wrap or waxed paper to prevent a skin from forming. Allow the custard to cool completely.

Once cool, stir in the cream and churn in an ice cream maker, according to the manufacturer's instructions. Serve immediately or transfer to a freezer container, cover the surface directly with waxed paper or foil and put in the freezer.

Milk chocolate ice cream

Dark chocolate ice cream

Dark chocolate ice cream

Velvet

This recipe was inspired by Italian food writer Marcella Hazan's Chocolate Gelato, first published in her book *Marcella's Kitchen*. It's dark, velvety and divine.

Makes 2½ cups (600ml)

4 large egg yolks
½ cup (100g) plus 2 Tbsp **extra-fine sugar**
2¼ cups (500ml) **whole milk**
3½oz (100g) **bittersweet chocolate (70% cocoa solids)** broken into pieces
½ cup (50g) **unsweetened cocoa**

In a heatproof bowl, beat (using an electric whisk) the egg yolks with ½ cup (100g) sugar until thick and creamy. Gently heat the milk in a saucepan to near-boiling point, then pour into the bowl with the egg mixture, beating well.

Melt the chocolate in a heatproof bowl over a saucepan of simmering water. Beat the melted chocolate into the egg mixture, followed by the cocoa. Place the bowl over a pan of simmering water and stir with a wooden spoon until the bubbles deflate and the mixture coats the back of the spoon. Remove from the heat. Meanwhile, in a small saucepan, make a caramel by combining 2 tablespoons of sugar with 2 tablespoons of water. Boil the mixture until it turns dark amber in color, swirling the saucepan as it darkens. When it reaches 350°F (180°C) on a sugar thermometer, it is ready.

Whisk the caramel into the chocolate until smooth; it will sizzle. Cover the surface with plastic wrap and cool. Leave in the refrigerator for at least 1 hour, then churn in an ice cream maker, according to the manufacturer's instructions. Serve or transfer to a freezer container, cover the surface with waxed paper or foil and put in the freezer.

Coffee ice cream

Sophisticated

Use freshly brewed espresso or cafetière coffee for this recipe if you can – the difference is astounding. Instant coffee is given as an alternative, but the flavor will, inevitably, not be as intense. If you are a true coffee lover, you may find the end result disappointing.

Makes 3¼ cups (800ml)

⅔ cup (150ml) **espresso coffee or** 2 tsp **instant coffee** dissolved in ⅔ cup (150ml) boiling water
⅔ cup (150ml) **whole milk**
½ cup (100g) **light brown sugar**
5 **large egg yolks**
1¼ cups (300ml) **heavy cream**

Combine the coffee and milk and allow it to cool slightly.

In a heatproof bowl, beat the sugar and egg yolks, using an electric whisk, until thick and pale. Stir in the milk mixture and place the bowl over a saucepan of simmering water. Continue stirring until the mixture is thick enough to coat the back of a wooden spoon. Remove from the heat, cover and allow to cool.

Stir in the heavy cream and churn in an ice cream maker, according to the manufacturer's instructions. Serve immediately or transfer to a freezer container, cover the surface directly with waxed paper or foil and put in the freezer.

■ *Variation: stir ¼ cup (50g) coarsely ground coffee beans into the ice cream just before freezing.*

Coffee ice cream

Caramel ice cream

Divine

If you're looking for a top-quality ice cream, look no further. This is rich, smooth and full of depth – frozen sophistication.

Makes 2½ cups (600ml)

1 cup (200g) **extra-fine sugar**
6 Tbsp (75ml) **water**
1 **vanilla bean**
1½ cups (375ml) **heavy cream**
1 cup (250ml) **whole milk**
6 **large egg yolks**

Combine the sugar and water in a heavy-bottomed saucepan. Split the vanilla bean lengthwise, scrape out the seeds with the back of a knife, and add both seeds and bean to the sugar and water. Heat gently over medium-low heat until the sugar dissolves. Increase the heat and gently boil the mixture, without stirring, until the mixture becomes deep amber in color, approximately 8 minutes, with a temperature of 350°F (180°C) on a sugar thermometer. Remove the saucepan from the heat and add the cream – there will be lots of bubbles – and stir until the caramel dissolves. Return the saucepan to a low heat, add the milk and simmer gently.

Using an electric beater, whisk the egg yolks in a separate bowl. Remove the vanilla bean from the cream mixture and slowly pour the cream mixture over the yolks, whisking constantly. Return the mixture to the saucepan and continue whisking over low heat until it is thick enough to coat the back of a wooden spoon. Strain the mixture into a clean bowl and cover the surface with plastic wrap. Cool, then refrigerate for 1 hour before churning in an ice cream maker, according to the manufacturer's instructions. Serve immediately or transfer to a freezer container and cover the surface directly with waxed paper or foil and freeze.

Caramel ice cream

Dinner parties

As we've established, cooking for friends is an opportunity to show off. Consider Antonin Carême, the famous nineteenth-century French chef. He was a supreme show-off. Ice cream, he believed, was the perfect medium in which to do so – he could mold it to his own architectural specifications, freeze it, then decorate it as he pleased. This effort was intended entirely to delight dinner guests before they demolished his creations.

You, too, can dazzle your guests with edible edifices if you choose, but remember that taste, exciting flavors and fresh ingredients are key to making memorable creations.

This chapter will equip you with a variety of crowd pleasers – from rich, show-stopping ice creams, to a delicate trio of sorbets or a sophisticated semifreddo. Many of the sorbets are also designed to be served between courses, either to cleanse the palate or to create unique flavor combinations in the mouth in conjunction with other dishes served.

The following recipes shouldn't be limited to the realm of entertaining – there's always room in life simply to impress yourself.

party-trick ices

Baileys® and macadamia semifreddo
Mellow

Baileys® Irish cream combined with the creamy texture of macadamia nuts is the ultimate dinner party indulgence. Serve a short espresso on the side to counterbalance the sweetness or, if you prefer, a shot of Baileys®.

Makes 2½ cups (600ml)

6 large egg yolks
½ cup (100g) extra-fine sugar
½ cup (100ml) Baileys® Irish cream
1¼ cups (300ml) heavy cream
1 cup (100g) macadamia nuts
  chopped

Using an electric whisk, beat the egg yolks and sugar in a heatproof bowl over a saucepan of simmering water until pale and creamy. Slowly add the Baileys® and beat until well combined and thick. Remove the bowl from the heat and continue beating until cool.

In a separate bowl, whip the cream until stiff peaks form. Fold the cream and macadamia nuts into the cooled Baileys® mixture, then transfer to a freezer container. Cover the surface directly with waxed paper or foil and freeze. After 1 hour of freezing, stir the mixture gently to prevent the macadamia nuts from sinking to the bottom. Cover again and freeze.

▦ *Variation: try this with walnuts, or any other nut.*

Chocolate and hazelnut swirl

Bittersweet

This rich, indulgent and velvety bittersweet ice cream is a
dinner party winner, guaranteed to wake up the taste buds.

Makes 2½ cups (600ml)

2½ cups (600ml) **Dark chocolate ice cream**
    unchurned (see page 33)
1 cup (100g) **hazelnuts**
    toasted and chopped
⅔ cup (150ml) **Chocolate fudge sauce** (see page 164)

Churn the dark chocolate ice cream in an ice cream maker,
according to the manufacturer's instructions, until just frozen. Stir
in the chopped hazelnuts.

Have ready a freezer container 1½ times the volume of the ice
cream (about 6¼ cups/1.5 liters in capacity). Spoon half of the ice
cream into the container. Add half of the chocolate fudge sauce
to the ice cream by spooning small amounts randomly over the
surface. Top with the remaining ice cream and sauce. Drag a
metal spoon three or four times through the ice cream to create a
swirling effect with the sauce. Cover the surface directly with
waxed paper or foil and freeze.

■ *Variation: try using other nuts or sauces to create the same effect, or swirl the
sauce and hazelnuts through Vanilla ice cream (see page 26).*

Tiramisu ice cream torta

Sophisticated

Tiramisu is Italian for "pick me up," and is a rich dessert
originally from Venice. This frozen version is a variation on the
traditional dessert and an impressive finish to any Italian meal.

Makes 4 cups (900ml)

1 cup (100g) **extra-fine sugar**
1¼ cups (300ml) **water**
1 Tbsp **instant coffee powder**
5oz (150g) **amaretti cookies or ladyfingers**
¼ cup (45ml) **Tia Maria®, marsala or dark rum**
1 cup (250ml) **heavy cream**
Scant 1 cup (200g) **mascarpone**

Line the base and sides of a loaf pan (9 x 4¾ x 2⅓in/
23 x 12 x 6cm) with waxed paper or foil and set aside.

Put the sugar, water and coffee powder in a saucepan and bring
to a boil, stirring constantly. Simmer for 5 minutes, uncovered,
then cool completely. Soak the amaretti cookies in the alcohol.

Whip the cream until stiff peaks form, then add the mascarpone
and beat until combined. Slowly stir the coffee syrup mixture into
the cream and continue beating until smooth.

Use a third of the soaked cookies to line the base of the pan.
Roughly crush the remaining cookies and fold through the coffee-
cream mixture. Pour the coffee-cream mixture over the amaretti.
Cover the surface directly with waxed paper or foil and put
in the freezer. To serve, remove the torta from the pan and cut
into slices. Serve sprinkled with unsweetened cocoa, if you like.

Tiramisu ice cream torta

Apricot and cardamom yogurt ice cream

Fragrant

Apricots go well with cardamom. The little black seeds inside the green cardamom pods give a strong but subtle flavor. With the addition of yogurt, this ice cream has an almost Indian slant.

Makes 3¼ cups (800ml)

2½ cups (500g) **fresh apricots**
1 cup (200g) **extra-fine sugar**
Scant 1 cup (200ml) **water**
3 **cardamom pods** lightly crushed
Juice of 1 **orange**
1¾ cups (400ml) **Greek yogurt**

Halve the apricots, remove the pits and chop. Put the chopped apricots, sugar, water, cardamom pods and orange juice in a large saucepan and bring to a boil. Cover and simmer until the fruit is tender, about 8–10 minutes. Remove the cardamom pods, transfer the mixture to a food processor and process until smooth. Allow to cool completely.

Stir the yogurt into the cooled mixture and churn in an ice cream maker, according to the manufacturer's instructions, until frozen. Transfer to an ice cream container or ice block molds and freeze. Put in the refrigerator 20 minutes before serving.

■ *If you're not a fan of cardamom and omit it, you're left with a delicious creamy apricot ice cream all on its own.*

Cinnamon and mascarpone ice cream

Spiced

Although very similar in texture to a thick cream, mascarpone is an Italian cheese. Its creaminess makes it a perfect ice cream ingredient.

Makes 3¼ cups (800ml)

1¼ cups (200g) **brown sugar**
1½ cups (350ml) **water**
1½ tsp **ground cinnamon**
1¾ cups (400g) **mascarpone**
⅔ cup (150ml) **heavy cream** lightly whipped

Heat the sugar and water in a medium saucepan over medium heat until the sugar has dissolved. Bring to a boil, then simmer, uncovered, for 10 minutes. Remove from the heat, stir in the cinnamon and allow it to cool completely.

Combine the syrup, mascarpone and cream and place in a freezer container. Cover the surface with waxed paper or foil and put in the freezer. Alternatively, do not whip the cream, and churn the combined mixture using an ice cream maker, according to the manufacturer's instructions. Cover the surface directly with waxed paper or foil and freeze.

■ *Try adding mixed spices, nutmeg or even ground cardamom, instead of cinnamon.*

Nougat ice cream

Nougat ice cream

Tropical

Be careful when boiling the sugar, glucose and honey – the mixture gets hot! It is important to work fast once your egg whites are beaten and to pour the syrup in steadily, beating constantly until cool. You'll be impressed with the outcome.

Makes 6¼ cups (1.5L)

¼ cup (75g) **extra-fine sugar**
¼ cup (50ml) **liquid glucose syrup**
¼ cup (50ml) **honey**
6 **large egg whites** (see note on page 4)
1¼ cups (300ml) **heavy cream**
  lightly whipped
Scant 1 cup (200g) **dried mixed tropical fruit**
  chopped
¾ cup (100g) **slivered almonds**

Place the sugar, glucose and honey in a saucepan. Bring to a simmer and stir once or twice until the sugar has dissolved. Once the sugar has dissolved, bring to a boil and continue boiling until the mixture reaches 240°F (116°C) on a sugar thermometer.

When the syrup is nearly ready, beat the egg whites, using an electric whisk, until stiff peaks form. With the whisk still running, pour the syrup on to the egg whites and continue beating until cool. Fold the lightly whipped cream into the cool nougat mix, then fold in the fruit and nuts.

Pour the mixture into a 2-quart (2-liter) loaf pan lined with baking parchment or foil and smooth the top using a spatula. Cover the surface and freeze. When the ice cream is frozen, carefully unmold it and serve cut into slices.

Mini chocolate semifreddo logs

Decadent

This semifreddo looks great made in small loaf pans – you will need eight 4 x 2in (10 x 5cm) pans. Everyone feels special getting their own ice cream mold at a dinner party – it's well worth it. You can make the semifreddo in one larger loaf pan (9 x 4¾ x 2⅓in/23 x 12 x 6cm).

Makes 8 small logs

3 **large eggs** (see note on page 4)
    separated
Scant ½ cup (125g)
    extra-fine sugar
Scant ½ cup (200g)
    mascarpone
    beaten
1 Tbsp **pure vanilla paste or vanilla extract**
Finely grated zest of 1 **lemon**
¼ cup (60g) **extra-fine sugar**
2oz (60g) **semisweet chocolate**
    finely grated

Line the base and sides of each pan with foil. Leave enough overhang to enable you to unmold the ice cream easily, once frozen.

Beat the egg yolks and ¼ cup (60g) of the sugar, using an electric whisk, in a heatproof bowl over a saucepan of simmering water until thick, pale and creamy. Remove the bowl from the heat and beat for 1 more minute. Add the mascarpone, vanilla paste and lemon zest and beat until just combined. Set aside.

Beat the egg whites in a separate bowl until soft peaks form. Gradually beat in the remaining sugar until it is combined and the mixture looks glossy, with soft peaks. Fold the egg whites gently into the mascarpone mixture.

Fill each loaf pan half full. Stir the chocolate into the remaining mixture and top off the loaf pans. Cover with foil and freeze for 4–6 hours for small pans (or overnight for one large pan). Unmold before serving and decorate with bought or homemade chocolate curls, if you like.

Mini chocolate semifreddo logs

Zabaglione ice cream

Creamy

Zabaglione, the classic Sicilian dessert, is a perennial favorite in the Italian culinary repertoire. It makes an excellent ice cream.

Makes 2½ cups (600ml)

6 **large egg yolks**
¾ cup (100g) **light brown sugar**
½ cup (100ml) **marsala**
1¼ cups (300ml) **heavy cream**
½ tsp **vanilla extract**

Beat the egg yolks and sugar, using an electric whisk, in a heatproof bowl over a saucepan of simmering water, until thick, pale and creamy (about 10 minutes). Slowly add the marsala and beat until well combined and thick. Remove the bowl from the heat and continue beating until the mixture is cool.

In a separate bowl, whip the cream with the vanilla until stiff peaks form. Fold the whipped cream into the cooled marsala mixture, then transfer to a freezer container. Cover the surface directly with waxed paper or foil and freeze.

■ *This is delicious served with thin crispy cookies, biscotti or amaretti.*

Goat cheese and honey ice cream
Semisweet

This recipe is based on the goat cheese sorbet served at one of Auckland's finest restaurants – Vinnies. Here, we have added honey and reduced the amount of cheese to produce a sweeter end product. It may sound strange, but this is delicious served with raspberries or blackberries and drizzled with extra lavender honey.

Makes 2¼ cups (500ml)

¾ cup (150g) **extra-fine sugar**
1 cup (250ml) **water**
Juice of 1 **lemon**
4–5 Tbsp (45–50ml) **lavender honey or any honey of your choice**
Scant ½ cup (100g) **soft goat cheese (preferably low in salt)**
½ cup (100ml) **sour cream**

Put the sugar, water, lemon juice and honey in a saucepan and bring to a boil. Reduce the heat and simmer for 5 minutes. Cool completely.

Once the syrup is cool, put the goat cheese and sour cream in a food processor with half the syrup and process until smooth. Press through a sieve and stir in the remaining syrup.

Churn in an ice cream maker, according to the manufacturer's instructions, for about 10 minutes, or until the mixture has the consistency of lightly whipped cream. Transfer to a freezer container and cover the surface directly with waxed paper or foil and freeze.

Bittersweet cocoa sorbet

Bittersweet cocoa sorbet

Indulgent

This bittersweet sorbet is not for the fainthearted. Lovers of fine bitter chocolate will adore this, but those who like their chocolate a little sweeter may find this rather intense. Use the finest quality cocoa you can buy, and serve the sorbet with a glass of your best brandy for added pleasure.

Makes 3¼ cups (800ml)

1¼ cups (275g) **extra-fine sugar**
1 quart (1L) **water**
1 cup (125g) **unsweetened cocoa**
   sifted
1 Tbsp **pure vanilla paste or vanilla extract**

Put the sugar and water in a medium saucepan and bring to a boil. Add the cocoa and stir until well combined. Bring the mixture back to a boil. Reduce the heat and simmer for 20 minutes over low heat, stirring occasionally. Cover and cool the mixture completely, then add the vanilla paste.

Churn in an ice cream maker, according to the manufacturer's instructions, for about 20 minutes, or until the mixture is frozen. Serve immediately in small bowls, or transfer to a freezer container, cover the surface directly with waxed paper or foil and put in the freezer. Remove from the freezer 15 minutes before serving to allow to soften slightly.

■ *You can add a couple of teaspoons of ground cinnamon to the sorbet if you like a little spice. This ice cream is great served with Crispy almond and lemon triangles (see page 173).*

Strawberry and balsamic vinegar sorbet

Aromatic

Balsamic vinegar may seem an unlikely addition to ice cream, but if you have tried this combination before, you will know that it works. This rich, sweet and fragrant vinegar perfectly complements lush, juicy strawberries.

Makes 2½ cups (600ml)

3¼ cups (500g) **strawberries**
    hulled
Juice of 1 **lemon**
¾ cup (150g) **extra-fine sugar**
1¼ cups (300ml) **water**
2 Tbsp **balsamic vinegar**
2 **egg whites** (see note on page 4)
    lightly beaten with a fork

Put the strawberries, lemon juice, sugar, water and balsamic vinegar in a large saucepan and bring to a boil. Reduce the heat and simmer, uncovered, for 5 minutes. Cool slightly, then transfer to a food processor and process to a smooth purée. Cover and allow to cool completely.

Churn the mixture in an ice cream maker, according to the manufacturer's instructions, for 10 minutes before adding the egg whites. Continue to churn until frozen. Serve immediately or transfer to a freezer container. Cover the surface directly with waxed paper or foil and put in the freezer. Remove from the freezer 15 minutes before serving to allow to soften slightly.

■ *If you are using the finest of balsamic vinegars, then splash a few tiny droplets over your sorbet when serving.*

Raspberry and kaffir lime leaf sorbet

Fragrant

Kaffir lime leaves can be bought from your local Thai or Asian supermarket. Buy more than you need and freeze them in a freezer bag until required. They impart a unique flavor to a traditional raspberry sorbet.

Makes 2½ cups (600ml)

2 cups (450g) **fresh raspberries**
¾ cup (150g) **extra-fine sugar**
1¼ cups (300ml) **water**
Juice of 1 **lime**
3–4 **fresh or frozen kaffir lime leaves**

Put all the ingredients in a medium saucepan and bring to a boil. Reduce the heat and simmer for 5 minutes. Remove from the heat and cool for 5–10 minutes. Remove the kaffir lime leaves from the cooled mixture and transfer the mixture to a food processor. Process to a purée, then strain through a sieve to remove the raspberry seeds. Refrigerate until the syrup has cooled completely.

When the syrup is cold, churn in an ice cream maker, according to the manufacturer's instructions, until frozen. Serve immediately or transfer to a freezer container and cover the surface directly with waved paper or foil and put in the freezer. Remove from the freezer 15 minutes before serving to allow to soften slightly.

■ *Variation: if you can't find kaffir lime leaves, try using a few mint leaves instead. Raspberry sorbet on its own is quite special, too. Scatter some fresh raspberries or other berries over the sorbet before serving.*

Chocolate-dipped ice cream morsels

Seductive

These are the perfect way to finish a meal when you don't feel like serving a full dessert. Rum and raisin ice cream (see page 142) dipped in bitter, dark chocolate works very well, but try any combination you like.

Makes about 16

1¼ cups (300ml) **ice cream of your choice**
7oz (200g) **semisweet chocolate**

Using a small ice cream scoop or melon baller, shape the ice cream into small balls. Place on parchment-lined baking sheets and place in the freezer until frozen hard.

Melt the chocolate over a saucepan of simmering water or in the microwave. Allow to cool but not set.

Dip the frozen ice cream balls, using two spoons, into the cooled chocolate, and return the balls to the lined sheets. Repeat until all the balls are dipped. Freeze until you are ready to serve.

■ *Variation: children will enjoy Peppermint chocolate chip (see page 127) morsels dipped in white chocolate or Coconut ice cream (see page 83) dipped in semisweet chocolate. Try adding food coloring to white chocolate for colored morsels, or dip the coated morsels in chopped nuts or dry unsweetened coconut.*

Chocolate-dipped ice cream morsels

Lime ice cream

Tart

This tart ice cream, reminiscent of a daiquiri, is made without the use of an ice cream maker.

Makes 3 cups (700ml)

1¼ cups (300ml) **heavy cream**
1¼ cups (300ml) **whole milk**
1 cup (200g) **extra-fine sugar**
6 Tbsp (75ml) **lime juice**
Grated zest of 1 **lime**

Combine the cream, milk and ½ cup (125g) sugar in a saucepan and heat gently, stirring occasionally until the sugar dissolves. Cool, then pour into an airtight container and place in the freezer.

Meanwhile, combine the remaining sugar, lime juice and zest in a small saucepan and heat over low heat until the sugar dissolves. Increase the heat slightly and gently boil the mixture until it is fragrant and slightly thickened. Cool completely.

Pour the lime syrup into a small, airtight container and place in the freezer. When it just begins to freeze, remove the cream mixture from the freezer, and stir the slushy lime syrup through it. Cover the surface directly with waxed paper or foil, then return to the freezer.

■ *Variation: this can be made in exactly the same way using lemon juice.*

Caribbean banana and rum ice cream

Mature

This decadent ice cream is best made with very ripe, brown bananas and the best-quality dark rum you can find.

Makes 3¼ cups (800ml)

2¼ cups (500ml) **heavy cream**
1 cup (250ml) **whole milk**
3 **large egg yolks**
Scant 1 cup (150g) **brown sugar**
3 **ripe bananas**
Juice of 1 **lemon**
3–4 Tbsp **dark rum to taste**

Combine the cream and milk in a medium saucepan and heat gently to near-boiling point.

In a separate, heatproof bowl, beat the egg yolks and sugar until thick and pale. Gradually, using an electric whisk, stir in the hot cream and milk. Place the bowl over a saucepan of simmering water and continue stirring until the mixture is thick enough to coat the back of a wooden spoon. Remove the bowl from the heat and leave to cool over a bowl of ice, whisking occasionally.

When the custard is completely cold, whisk in the mushy bananas, lemon juice and rum to taste. Churn in an ice cream maker, according to the manufacturer's instructions. Transfer to a freezer container and cover the surface directly with waxed paper or foil before freezing.

Maple syrup and blueberry ice cream
Delicious

In this dessert, a creamy maple syrup ice cream is swirled through with blueberry compôte to make a colorful and delicious combination.

Makes 1 quart (1L)

2¼ cups (500ml) **whole milk**
1 **vanilla bean**
split in half lengthwise
6 **large egg yolks**
1 cup (250ml) **maple syrup**
1¼ cups (300ml) **Blueberry compôte** (see page 166)
2¼ cups (500ml) **heavy cream**

Put the milk and vanilla bean in a heavy-bottomed saucepan and heat to near-boiling point, stirring occasionally. Remove from the heat.

Meanwhile, in a heatproof bowl, beat the egg yolks, using an electric whisk, until thick and pale. Slowly beat in the syrup until combined.

Remove the vanilla bean from the milk, scraping out the seeds, and gradually beat the milk into the egg and maple syrup mixture. Place the bowl over a saucepan of simmering water and continue stirring until the mixture is thick enough to coat the back of a wooden spoon. Remove the bowl from the heat and cover the surface directly with plastic wrap to prevent a skin from forming. Allow the custard to cool completely.

Once cool, stir in the cream and churn in an ice cream maker, according to the manufacturer's instructions.

Spoon the ice cream and compôte into a container in alternate layers. Using a blunt knife, cut through the layers and carefully swirl the compôte through the ice cream. Cover the surface directly with waxed paper or foil and freeze.

Blonde rocky road
Sinful

A gooey, crunchy, sweet, decadent blonde version of Traditional rocky road ice cream (see page 124).

Makes 2½ cups (600ml)

1 cup (250ml) **whole milk**
2 **large egg yolks**
¼ cup (50g) **extra-fine sugar**
3½oz (100g) **white chocolate** broken into small pieces
⅔ cup (150ml) **heavy cream**
1 cup (100g) **macadamia nuts** toasted
1 cup (250ml) **Marshmallow sauce** (see page 164)

Place the milk in a medium saucepan and heat gently to near-boiling point.

In a separate heatproof bowl, beat the egg yolks and sugar, using an electric whisk, until thick and pale. Gradually beat the milk into the egg mixture. Place the bowl over a saucepan of simmering water and continue stirring until the mixture is thick enough to coat the back of a wooden spoon. Remove the bowl from the heat and mix in the chocolate pieces, stirring until smooth. Cover the surface directly with plastic wrap to prevent a skin from forming. Cool completely.

Once cool, stir in the cream and churn in an ice cream maker, according to the manufacturer's instructions. Stir in the nuts just before the ice cream sets. Spoon the ice cream and marshmallow sauce into a container in alternate layers. Using a blunt knife, cut through the layers and carefully swirl the sauce through the ice cream. Cover with waxed paper or foil and freeze.

Toasted hazelnut tortoni

Sweet

The classic biscuit tortoni is a frozen dessert traditionally made with sweetened whipped cream, stiff egg whites, chopped nuts and flavored with spirits. This version comes from Canada, where my friend Cynthia Shupe served it to me years ago. It is still a favorite.

Makes 6 servings of 1 cup (250ml) each

2 large egg whites (see note on page 4)
¼ tsp cream of tartar
¼ cup (60g) extra-fine sugar
1¾ cups (375ml) heavy cream
1 tsp vanilla extract
¼ cup (60ml) Grand Marnier
4 Tbsp dry unsweetened coconut
  toasted
½ cup (60g) hazelnuts
  toasted and chopped
3½oz (100g) bittersweet chocolate (70% cocoa solids)
  shaved

Beat the egg whites with the cream of tartar, using an electric whisk until soft peaks form. Add the sugar and beat until stiff peaks form.

In a separate bowl, whip the cream just until soft. Beat in the vanilla and Grand Marnier. In a small bowl, combine the coconut, hazelnuts and chocolate. Reserve a quarter of the mixture for garnish, and stir the remaining mixture into the cream. Combine the whipped cream and egg whites, and stir gently until smooth.

Place the tortoni in glasses and top with the reserved topping. Freeze for at least 4 hours. Alternatively, freeze the tortoni in a freezer container and spoon into dessert bowls to serve.

Toasted hazelnut tortoni

Ricotta ice cream with pine nuts

Ricotta ice cream with pine nuts
Toasted crunch

This recipe was inspired by a ricotta ice cream devised by Martha Stewart, which can be found in her voluminous book, *The Martha Stewart Cookbook*. In our recipe, we top the ice cream with toasted pine nuts and a drizzle of honey. The result is a creamy ice cream studded with a toasted crunch.

Makes 2 quarts (2L)

4 **large eggs** (see note on page 4)
½ cup (150g) **extra-fine sugar**
⅔ cup (150ml) **honey** plus 2 Tbsp **for drizzling**
1 tsp **vanilla extract**
2¼ cups (500g) **ricotta**
2¼ cups (500ml) **whole milk**
2¼ cups (500ml) **heavy cream** softly whipped
½ cup (50g) **pine nuts** toasted

Beat the eggs, sugar and honey, using an electric whisk, until thick and pale, about 6–8 minutes. Stir in the vanilla, ricotta, milk and whipped cream. Continue to beat for 2 minutes until smooth and thick.

Spread the mixture in a 13 x 8-in (33 x 22-cm) parchment-lined baking sheet with sides or a freezer container. Top with toasted pine nuts and a drizzle of honey. Cover the surface loosely with waxed paper or foil before freezing.

■ *Experiment with flavored honeys – lavender, orange blossom or rosemary will add a subtle touch to this ice cream.*

Ice cream affogato

Bitter sweetness

This is our version of the Italian *affogato* – gelato drowned in espresso. We love it with crisp Lemon and hazelnut biscotti (see page 172).

Serves 4

8 scoops **Vanilla and/or Coffee ice cream**
  (see pages 26 and 34)
2 Tbsp **coffee beans**
  finely ground
1¼ cups (300ml) **hot espresso coffee**

Divide the ice cream scoops between four glass cups or small bowls. Sprinkle with ground coffee beans and bring the cups to the table. Once there, pour coffee over each serving.

■ *Variation: try adding a splash of liqueur to this, such as Tia Maria®, Cointreau or brandy, for an after-dinner treat.*

Ice cream affogato

Kahlua®, walnut and chocolate swirl

Sophisticated

When you fancy a little something after dinner, but can't choose between a glass of the coffee-flavored liqueur Kahlua or a dessert, this ice cream is the answer.

Makes 3 cups (750ml)

1¼ cups (300ml) **whole milk**
4 **large egg yolks**
½ cup (100g) **extra-fine sugar**
1 tsp **vanilla extract**
1¼ cups (300ml) **heavy cream**
⅔ cup (150ml) **Kahlua®**
1 cup (100g) **walnuts**
   toasted and chopped
1½ cups (350ml) **Chocolate fudge sauce** (see page 164)

Place the milk in a medium saucepan and heat gently to near-boiling point. Remove the saucepan from the heat.

In a separate, heatproof bowl, beat the egg yolks, sugar and vanilla extract, using an electric whisk, until thick and pale. Gradually beat the milk into the egg mixture. Place the bowl over a saucepan of simmering water and continue stirring until the mixture is thick enough to coat the back of a wooden spoon. Remove the bowl from the heat and cover the surface directly with plastic wrap.

Once cool, stir in the cream and Kahlua® and churn in an ice cream maker, according to the manufacturer's instructions, until set.

Spoon the ice cream, nuts and sauce into a freezer container in alternate spoonfuls, giving an even distribution. Using a blunt knife, cut through the layers and carefully swirl the nuts and sauce through the ice cream. Cover the surface directly and freeze.

Blackberry cabernet sauvignon sorbet

Refreshing

Full of depth and fruity sweetness, this sorbet makes a perfect palate-cleanser between courses or a refreshing dessert. Serve with Candied kumquats (see page 169).

Makes 2¼ cups (500ml)

1 cup (200g) **extra-fine sugar**
½ cup (100ml) **water**
1 **vanilla bean**
2½ cups (600ml) **Cabernet Sauvignon**
1 cup (275g) **fresh or frozen blackberries (don't thaw if frozen)**
2 Tbsp **lemon juice**

Combine the sugar and water in a heavy-bottomed saucepan. Split the vanilla bean lengthwise, scrape out the seeds with the back of a knife, and add both seeds and bean to the sugar and water. Bring to a boil, then simmer the mixture without stirring, until it becomes slightly golden in color. Remove the saucepan from the heat and add the wine – there will be lots of bubbles – then return the saucepan to a low heat and stir until the caramel dissolves.

Add the blackberries and lemon juice and simmer gently for about 15 minutes, stirring occasionally and crushing the berries with a spoon. Remove from the heat and strain the mixture through a fine sieve, pushing as much juice as possible through with the back of a spoon. Allow the mixture to cool, then chill for at least 2 hours before churning in an ice cream maker, according to the manufacturer's instructions.

Serve, or spoon it into a freezer container, cover with a layer of waxed paper or baking parchment, cover and put in the freezer. Remove the sorbet from the freezer 15 minutes before serving, to allow it to soften slightly.

Lemongrass sorbet

Citronella

This delicate sorbet is almost like frozen lemonade, but carries an elusive citronella quality that gives it an extra-special flavor.

Makes 2¼ cups (500ml)

For the lemongrass syrup:
8 stalks **lemongrass**
6 Tbsp **extra-fine sugar**
6 Tbsp **water**

For the sorbet:
1¼ cups (300ml) **water**
⅔ cup (150ml) **lemon juice**
3 Tbsp **extra-fine sugar**
  or to taste

Bruise the lemongrass stalks by crushing them under the flat side of a chef's knife – this will release their flavor. Cut the bruised stalks into 2-in (5-cm) pieces.

Combine the lemongrass, sugar and water in a small, heavy-bottomed saucepan and bring to a boil. Reduce the heat and simmer until the syrup is slightly thickened (almost the texture of warm honey), for about 10 minutes. Remove from the heat and cool completely. When cool, strain the syrup and discard the lemongrass.

Combine the water and lemon juice in a bowl. Slowly stir in the sugar, one tablespoon at a time, until the liquid is sweet, but slightly tart. Stir in the cooled, strained syrup and taste. The mixture should be quite sweet – if not, add a little more sugar, keeping in mind that freezing will dull the sweetness of the sorbet. Chill the mixture for at least 1 hour, then churn in an ice cream maker, according to the manufacturer's instructions. Transfer to a freezer container, cover the surface directly with waxed paper or foil and freeze for at least 4 hours.

Thai basil sorbet

Licorice

Thai basil, found in Asian supermarkets, gives a gentle licoricelike flavor when sweetened and churned into a sorbet. It is a perfect ending to any Southeast Asian meal, or a refreshing accompaniment to a citrus salad.

Makes 2½ cups (600ml)

1 cup (200g) **extra-fine sugar**
Scant 1 cup (200ml) **water**
1 cup (50g) **Thai basil**
1 Tbsp **lime juice**
Orange segments to serve

Combine the sugar, water and basil in a heavy-bottomed saucepan over medium heat. Bring to a boil and simmer for 5 minutes. Remove the saucepan from the heat and leave to cool.

Strain the cooled syrup into a measuring jar and discard the Thai basil. Add water until the mixture measures 2½ cups (600ml), then stir in the lime juice.

Chill the mixture for 1 hour, then churn in an ice cream maker, according to the manufacturer's instructions. Spoon straight from the maker into serving bowls, or transfer to a freezer container, cover the surface directly with waxed paper or foil and put in the freezer. Remove from the freezer 15 minutes before serving to allow the sorbet to soften.

Serve with orange segments, if desired.

■ *Variation: if you substitute regular basil for Thai basil, also substitute lemon juice for lime.*

Clementine and star anise sorbet

Aniseed

This delicate, yet full-of-flavor creation is truly unique.

Makes 2¼ cups (500ml)

1 cup (250ml) **water**
½ cup (100g) **extra-fine sugar**
3 **whole star anise**
1 **vanilla bean**
2¼ cups (500ml) **fresh clementine juice**
Pinch of salt

Combine the water, sugar and star anise in a heavy-bottomed saucepan. Split the vanilla bean lengthwise, and add to the saucepan. Bring the mixture to a boil, then simmer for 5 minutes. Remove the saucepan from the heat and leave to cool.

When cool, strain and discard the spices. Stir the syrup into the clementine juice and add a pinch of salt.

Churn in an ice cream maker, according to the manufacturer's instructions. This sorbet is best eaten straight from the maker. If you are making it in advance, however, spoon the sorbet into a freezer container, cover with baking parchment or waxed paper and put in the freezer. Remove from the freezer 15 minutes before serving to allow the sorbet to soften slightly.

■ *Freshly squeezed orange juice can be substituted for the clementine juice.*

Clementine and star anise sorbet

Coffee granita

Coffee granita
Indulgent

This recipe is based on a dessert served at the Zuni Café in San Francisco. The sweet, icy coffee layered between whipped cream makes a simple, attractively cool dessert.

Makes 6 servings of 1 cup (250ml) each

For the granita:
1 cup (200g) **extra-fine sugar or to taste**
2¼ cups (500ml) **strong espresso coffee**
  cooled
3 Tbsp **water**

For the cream layer:
½ cup (125ml) **heavy cream**
2 Tbsp **extra-fine sugar**

To make the granita, slowly add sugar to the coffee, tasting continually until the coffee is very sweet. Add the water and stir well. Pour the mixture into a shallow metal bowl, dish or even a skillet – whatever will make it easiest for you to break up the ice crystals. Cover with foil and freeze until solid, about 8 hours.

Once solid, remove the granita from the freezer and, using a metal pastry scraper, break up the granita into small, irregular shards. Transfer to a chilled, airtight freezer container with a lid, close it and return the granita to the freezer.

Half an hour before serving, invert the container to distribute the syrup throughout the shards of ice. Chill glasses or glass bowls – whatever will show off the layers best.

Whip the cream and sugar in a bowl until stiff. Layer cream and granita in the serving glasses, finishing with a layer of granita.

Cranberry cosmo sorbet

Urban

A sharp, elegant sorbet that looks best served in a martini glass bathed in a splash of vodka.

Makes 2½ cups (600ml)

1½ cups (315g) **extra-fine sugar**

2¼ cups (500ml) **water**

2¾ cups (675g) **fresh or frozen cranberries (don't thaw if frozen)**

¼ cup (60ml) **lime juice**

2 Tbsp **fresh orange juice**

Grated zest of 1 **orange**

Combine the sugar and water in a saucepan over medium heat, stirring until the sugar has dissolved and the liquid begins to boil. Add the cranberries and simmer until the berries pop and collapse, about 12–15 minutes. Remove the saucepan from the heat and gently strain the berries into a bowl, pushing on them with the back of a spoon to extract as much juice as possible. Cover the liquid with plastic wrap, leave to cool and then place in the refrigerator.

When the juice is completely chilled, stir in the lime juice, orange juice and zest. Churn in an ice cream maker, according to the manufacturer's instructions. Serve immediately or transfer to a freezer container, cover the surface directly with waxed paper or foil and put in the freezer.

Remove from the freezer 15 minutes before serving to allow to soften slightly. Serve topped with Candied citrus peel (see page 163).

■ *Variation: for an authentic cosmopolitan, use Cointreau (the orange-flavored liqueur) instead of orange juice. You can also stir ¼ cup (60ml) vodka into the sorbet with the lime, orange juice and zest, but it will take much longer for the sorbet to freeze – up to 2 days. It is easiest to serve the finished sorbet with a splash of vodka.*

Cranberry cosmo sorbet

Raspberry semifreddo hearts

Raspberry semifreddo hearts

Heavenly

This is very easy to make and doesn't require any churning. Try making different shapes depending on the occasion.

Makes 10 hearts
(1 quart/1L)

8oz (250g) **white chocolate** broken into pieces
5 **large egg yolks**
¾ cup (75g) **extra-fine sugar**
1¼ cups (300g) **fresh raspberries**
3½oz (100g) **white chocolate** chopped into chunks
1¼ cups (300ml) **heavy cream**
1 tsp **vanilla extract**

Line the base and sides of the molds with waxed paper or foil (unless you are using flexible plastic molds). Melt the first quantity of white chocolate and set aside. Using an electric beater, beat the egg yolks and sugar in a heatproof bowl over a saucepan of simmering water until thick and pale; this will take about 5 minutes. Remove from the heat and continue beating until cool. Gently fold the raspberries, cooled melted chocolate and white chocolate chunks into the egg mixture.

Beat the cream and vanilla extract until soft peaks form. Gently fold the raspberry/egg mixture into the cream, being careful not to crush the raspberries too much. Pour the mixture into the lined molds and cover the surface directly with more waxed paper or foil before still freezing (see page 17). Serve with fresh berries.

■ *If you'd rather, you can make the semifreddo in a loaf pan and cut it into slices.*

Al fresco

There is something magical about eating al fresco. Whether it's a picnic on the beach, dinner in the garden or on a terrace in a faraway place, when the day is perfect, food always tastes better outside. This is especially true when the food you are savoring captures the essence of your surroundings: a glistening bejeweled pomegranate in Egypt, kiwi fruit in New Zealand, wild blueberries in Nova Scotia, herbs from your own garden. This is when food is pure, simple and ripe for the taking.

However, travel is a luxury, and we can't control the weather. Even when the garden furniture is out, the sun is beaming down and you are holding a chilled bowl of lemon and sage sorbet in your hand, the skies can still cloud over. But not to worry, tastes and aromas can transport you to another time, another land, a sunny garden. Ices can capture these tastes, suspend them, make them last. So when it rains, close your eyes and enjoy apple and rosemary blended through frozen Greek yogurt, or a sweet sorbet fragranced with rose petals. Savor it. Before you know it, you'll be al fresco once again.

Caramelized fig and orange ice cream

Irresistible

There's nothing better than picking a fig straight from the tree and squishing it between your teeth. This ice cream is for those times when the fruits are in abundance.

Makes 2½ cups (600ml)

¾ cup (150g) **extra-fine sugar**
1 cup (200g) **ripe figs (about 8 figs)**
    chopped into about 8 pieces
Juice and grated zest of 2 **oranges**
⅔ cup (150ml) **heavy cream**
1¼ cups (300ml) **whole milk**
3 **large egg yolks**

Heat scant ½ cup (75g) of the sugar in a heavy-bottomed frying skillet, without stirring, until dissolved and starting to turn golden. Add the figs and orange juice and stir until they are combined and bubbling. Add the orange zest and cream and continue to bubble for 2–3 minutes. Remove from the heat and cool completely.

Bring the milk to near-boiling point in a heavy-bottomed saucepan. Meanwhile, using an electric whisk, beat the eggs with the remaining sugar in a heatproof bowl until thick and pale. Place over a saucepan of boiling water and stir in the warmed milk. Stir occasionally until the mixture is thick enough to coat the back of a wooden spoon. Remove from the heat and allow to cool completely.

Once cool, combine the fig mixture with the custard and churn in an ice cream maker, according to the manufacturer's instructions. Serve immediately or transfer to a freezer container, cover the surface directly with waxed paper and put in the freezer.

Coconut ice cream
Creamy

Coconut ice cream is definitely one for a hot summer's day. Whether it's in your backyard, on a beach along the Amalfi Coast or down a hot, sticky Bangkok street, it somehow hits the spot every time.

Makes 2½ cups (600ml)

1¼ cups (300ml) **whole milk**
2oz (60g) **creamed coconut**
¾ cup (100g) **confectioner's sugar**
4 **large egg yolks**
¼ cup (45g) **dry unsweetened coconut (optional)**
1¼ cups (300ml) **heavy cream**

Warm the milk in a medium saucepan to near-boiling point. Add the creamed coconut and stir until dissolved. Strain the warm coconut milk through a fine sieve or cheesecloth.

Beat the confectioner's sugar and egg yolks in a heatproof bowl, using an electric whisk, until thick and pale. Put the bowl over a saucepan of simmering water and gradually stir in the coconut milk. Stir occasionally until the mixture is thick enough to coat the back of a wooden spoon. Stir in the coconut, if using, and cool completely. Stir in the cream and churn in an ice cream maker, according to the manufacturer's instructions, until frozen. Transfer to a freezer container, cover the surface directly with waxed paper or foil and put in the freezer.

■ *See page 20 for how best to toast coconut and add this instead of dry unsweetened coconut for a more nutty texture.*

Apple and rosemary frozen yogurt
Crisp

This snowy-white dessert is gelatolike in texture and subtly scented with rosemary. The yogurt gives it a slight sharpness, making it the ultimate palate cleanser.

Makes 2½ cups (600ml)

Scant 1 cup (200ml) **water**
1¼ cups (300ml) **apple juice**
¾ cup (150g) **extra-fine sugar**
2–3 **large rosemary sprigs**
Scant 1 cup (200ml) **Greek yogurt**

Put the water, apple juice, sugar and rosemary in a saucepan and bring to a boil. Reduce the heat and simmer for 5 minutes. Allow to cool. When cool, gently whisk in the yogurt. Churn in an ice cream maker, according to the manufacturer's instructions, until frozen. Then, serve immediately or transfer to a freezer container, cover the surface directly with waxed paper or foil and put in the freezer. Serve with crystallized rosemary needles, in Easy maple syrup cones, if desired (see page 170).

■ *To crystallize rosemary, remove the needles from the woody stalk. Combine 1 cup (200g) extra-fine sugar with scant 1 cup (200ml) water in a saucepan and bring to a boil, until sugar dissolves. Add needles, reduce heat and simmer for 30 minutes. Remove needles with a slotted spoon and place on paper towels. When cool, toss the rosemary needles through another ½ cup (100g) extra-fine sugar.*

■ *To stand cones in glasses or bowls, pack out the base of the glass or bowl with soft brown sugar, insert the cones, and they will stand upright.*

Apple and rosemary frozen yogurt

Fresh mint ice cream

Clean

This fresh mint ice cream tastes almost like a creamy Moroccan mint tea. Whole eggs give it a smooth, special texture, while the chocolate, although optional, adds a lovely, rich bite. Fresh mint has never tasted better. (See page 134.)

Makes 3¼ cups (800ml)

2¼ cups (500ml) **heavy cream**
1 cup (250ml) **whole milk**
½ cup (30g) **fresh mint leaves**
¾ cup (150g) **extra-fine sugar**
2 **whole large eggs**
3½oz (100g) **bittersweet chocolate (70% cocoa solids)** chopped (optional)

Blend the cream, milk and fresh mint leaves in a blender. Pour into a heavy-bottomed saucepan and slowly heat to near-boiling point. Reduce the heat and cook gently, stirring occasionally, for 7 minutes. Remove from the heat, strain and allow to cool slightly.

Meanwhile, in a separate, heatproof bowl, beat the eggs and sugar, using an electric whisk, until thick and pale. Gradually beat the milk into the egg mixture. Place the bowl over a saucepan of simmering water and continue stirring until the mixture is thick enough to coat the back of a wooden spoon. Remove the bowl from the heat and cover the surface directly with plastic wrap or waxed paper to prevent a skin from forming. Allow the custard to cool completely before refrigerating for at least 1 hour.

Once chilled, churn in an ice cream maker, according to the manufacturer's instructions, stopping just before the ice cream has set (usually 5 minutes before completion). Stir in the chopped chocolate. Transfer to a freezer container, cover the surface directly with waxed paper or foil and put in the freezer.

Marmalade parfait

Zesty

Well, a parfait of sorts. French parfaits are frozen desserts made with ice cream, sweetened with fruit or fruit juices, and layered with whipped heavy cream. Our version twists the rules a little by adding whipped egg whites to lighten, and fine-cut marmalade to add a sophisticated, bittersweet twist.

Makes 3¼ cups (800ml)

2 **egg whites** (see note on page 4)
¼ tsp **cream of tartar**
2 Tbsp **extra-fine sugar**
1½ cups (350ml) **heavy cream**
1¼ cups (300g) **fine-cut tangerine and orange or other marmalade**
Grated zest of 1 **lemon**
Juice of ½ **lemon**
Grated zest of 1 **tangerine**

In a large bowl, beat the egg whites with the cream of tartar until soft peaks form. Add the sugar and beat until stiff peaks form. In a separate bowl, whip the cream just until soft peaks form. Stir in the marmalade, the lemon zest and juice and the tangerine zest.

Divide the mixture between 6 dessert glasses and freeze for at least 3 hours. Alternatively, transfer to a freezer container, cover the surface directly with waxed paper or foil and freeze. Spoon into bowls when ready to serve.

■ *This is attractive served in orange skins. Cut six oranges in half and carefully remove the segments from the bottom halves. Freeze the skins. When the parfait is ready, spoon it into the skins and serve with Candied citrus peel (see page 163).*

Lavender frozen yogurt

Floral

A delicately floral, creamy frozen yogurt that manages to be both sophisticated and comforting. Serve it on its own, or with crystallized lavender sprigs (see page 20).

Makes 1 quart (1L)

1 cup (200g) **extra-fine sugar**
Scant 1 cup (200ml) **water**
2 Tbsp **lavender buds**
1¼ cups (300ml) **Greek yogurt**
1¼ cups (300ml) **crème fraîche or sour cream**
Juice of 2 **limes**

Combine the sugar, water and lavender buds in a small, heavy-bottomed saucepan and bring to a boil, stirring occasionally. Reduce the heat and simmer the syrup for 2 minutes. Remove from the heat and allow to cool. Don't worry if your kitchen is overpowered by the smell of Granny's soap collection – the lavender aroma mellows beautifully when frozen. When the syrup is cool, strain and discard the lavender.

Combine the Greek yogurt and crème fraîche in a large bowl. Whisk in the lavender syrup and lime juice. Chill the mixture for 1 hour, then churn in an ice cream maker, according to the manufacturer's instructions. Serve immediately or transfer to a freezer container, cover the surface directly with waxed paper or foil and put in the freezer.

■ *Lavender buds are available from speciality or health food stores. Seek out organic varieties – if unavailable, rinse the buds before using.*

Lavender frozen yogurt

Rhubarb crumble ice cream
Creamy crunch

This delectable ice cream captures the essence of the finest of flavors and textures – raspberries, rhubarb and crisp, buttery crumble, all cradled in a cloud of sweet cream.

Makes 1 quart (1L)

For the ice cream:
12oz (350g) **rhubarb** chopped into ½-in (1-cm) pieces
½ cup (100g) **fresh or frozen raspberries (do not thaw)**
1 cup (200g) **extra-fine sugar**
1 Tbsp **lemon juice**
2 cups (450ml) **heavy cream**

For the crumble:
⅔ cup (75g) **all-purpose flour**
½ cup (50g) **rolled oats**
½ stick (50g) **butter**
⅓ cup (50g) **brown sugar**
½ tsp **ground ginger**

Preheat the oven to 375°F (190°C).

Combine the rhubarb, raspberries, sugar and lemon juice in a large, shallow baking dish. Put the fruit in the oven and bake for 20 minutes or until tender. Cool and blend until smooth.

Using your hands, combine the crumble ingredients in a bowl until it resembles coarse crumbs. Transfer to a baking dish and place in the preheated oven for 10 minutes, or until golden. Remove and break into small pieces. Cool.

Combine the cream and fruit purée in a large bowl. Churn in an ice cream maker, according to the manufacturer's instructions. Spoon the ice cream and crumble pieces into a freezer container in alternate layers. Using a blunt knife, gently cut through the layers, swirling the crumble throughout the ice cream. Cover the surface directly with waxed paper or foil and freeze for at least 3 hours.

Pineapple ice cream

Tropical

We have experimented with different versions of pineapple ice cream – adding molasses and cardamom or brown sugar and lime. But, at the end of the day, plain, simple old pineapple won, hands down!

Makes 3¼ cups (800ml)

1 quantity **Vanilla ice cream** (see page 26)
  made to the custard stage omitting the vanilla bean
1 **pineapple**
Juice of 1 **lime**

Make the vanilla ice cream to the custard stage (when mixture coats the back of a wooden spoon). Put the custard to chill in the refrigerator while you prepare the pineapple purée. Top and tail the pineapple, then peel and core it. Roughly chop and place the chunks in a bowl, together with any juices left on the cutting board. Purée the pineapple, using a hand-held blender. (Don't worry if small, pea-size bits of pineapple remain – they add texture and character to the ice cream.)

Take the custard out of the refrigerator. Stir in the pineapple purée and lime juice and churn in an ice cream maker, according to the manufacturer's instructions. Serve immediately or transfer to a freezer container, cover the surface directly with waxed paper or foil and put in the freezer.

Quince and goat milk frozen yogurt
Tart

Quince is a relative of the apple and the pear, but is too sour to eat raw. When heated, however, it has a delicious aroma and turns a lovely pink color. It is most commonly eaten as a preserve. Quince jelly is delicious with cheese, and equally good, we've discovered, paired with goat milk yogurt and frozen.

Makes 1 quart (1L)

1 cup (200g) **quince jelly**
½ cup (100ml) **apple juice**
2 Tbsp **honey**
1¼ cups (300ml) **goat milk yogurt**
1¼ cups (300ml) **crème fraîche or sour cream**
Juice of 1 **lemon**

Combine the quince jelly, apple juice and honey in a small, heavy-bottomed saucepan and bring to a boil, stirring occasionally. Reduce the heat and simmer for 2 minutes. Remove from heat and cool.

Combine the yogurt and crème fraîche in a large bowl. Whisk in the quince syrup and add the lemon juice. Chill the mixture for 1 hour, then churn in an ice cream maker, according to the manufacturer's instructions. Serve immediately or transfer to a freezer container, cover the surface directly with waxed paper or foil and put in the freezer.

■ *Quince jelly is available from most cheese stores or delicatessens.*

Kaffir lime and coconut ice cream

Citrus

Kaffir lime leaves, native to Southeast Asia and Hawaii, lend a unique citrus aroma to Asian dishes. Here, they flavor a unique ice cream.

Makes 3 cups (700ml)

½ cup (100g) **extra-fine sugar**
¾ cup (100g) **palm or brown sugar**
Scant 1 cup (200ml) **water**
10 **kaffir lime leaves** coarsely torn
1¾ cups (400ml) **canned coconut milk**
1 cup (250ml) **heavy cream**
Juice of 1 **lime**

Combine both sugars, water and leaves in a small, heavy-bottomed saucepan and bring to a boil, stirring occasionally. Reduce the heat and simmer the syrup for 2 minutes. Remove from the heat and cool. When the syrup is cool, strain and discard the torn leaves.

Combine the coconut milk and cream in a large bowl. Whisk in the syrup and lime juice. Chill the mixture for 1 hour, then churn in an ice cream maker, according to the manufacturer's instructions. Serve immediately or transfer to a freezer container, cover the surface directly with waxed paper or foil and put in the freezer.

■ *Look for kaffir lime leaves, either fresh or dried, in Asian markets. The leaves are best stored in an airtight container in the freezer.*

Rose petal sorbet
Turkish delight

A sorbet made with sparkling wine and rose petals – the perfect ending to a romantic meal.

Makes 3 cups (750ml)

2 Tbsp **dried organic rose petals**
1 cup (200g) **extra-fine sugar**
3 cups (750ml) **water**
3 Tbsp **lemon juice**
1 cup (250ml) **sparkling wine (such as Cava)**
1 Tbsp **rosewater or to taste**

Combine the rose petals, sugar and 1 cup (250ml) water in a heavy-bottomed saucepan over medium heat. Bring to a boil and simmer for 5 minutes. Remove from the heat and allow to cool completely.

Strain the cooled syrup through a sieve into a large bowl or measuring jar and discard the dried petals. Add the remaining ingredients (including the rest of the water), adding rosewater to taste. Churn in an ice cream maker, according to the manufacturer's instructions, until frozen. Serve immediately or transfer to a freezer container, cover with waxed paper or baking parchment, and put in the freezer. Remove from the freezer 15 minutes before serving to allow the sorbet to soften.

■ *Seek out dried rose petals in organic health food stores. If you can't find them, use ¾ cup (50g) fresh organic rose petals (don't use roses from your own garden if you use pesticides). If organic petals can't be found, flavor the sorbet just with rosewater, using up to 2–4 tablespoons to achieve the right flavor.*

Rose petal sorbet

Melon and chile sorbet

Piquant

Mexicans love to cool off with *paletas*, literally "little shovels" in Spanish, which are frozen treats on sticks. Some are creamy, made with milk and fruit or berries; others are icy, flavored with tart fruits or chile peppers. This sorbet is based on the latter – sweet melon with a hint of chile. This refreshing sorbet, with a surprising hint of heat, is quick and easy to make.

Makes 3 cups (750ml)

1 **cantaloupe melon**
¼ cup (60g) **extra-fine sugar**
Juice of 2 **lemons**
1 **red chile pepper** stalk and seeds removed

Cut through the melon, remove the seeds and skin, and chop the flesh. Combine all the ingredients in a blender and purée until smooth. Chill the mixture for 1 hour, then churn in an ice cream maker, according to the manufacturer's instructions.

Sorbets are best scooped straight out of the maker, but can be transferred to a freezer container and frozen. Before serving, allow the frozen sorbet to soften slightly to regain its slushy texture, about 15 minutes.

■ *Use fresh red chile peppers in this recipe. If you aren't sure how hot the chile is, add it slowly to the blended melon, tasting as you go. Bear in mind that the heat will reduce when the sorbet is frozen.*

Pear and bay leaf sorbet
Winter fresh

Finally, the glorious bay leaf can escape its savory status and feature in a sweet, refreshing sorbet. Its aroma is fresh yet wintry, which combines beautifully with pears. Try to use fresh bay leaves in this recipe – dried will do, but the flavor is not as intense.

Makes 3¼ cups (800ml)

4lb (2kg) **ripe pears**
1½ cups (350ml) **water**
1 cup (200g) **extra-fine sugar**
10–12 **fresh bay leaves**
2 Tbsp **lemon juice**

Peel, core and chop the pears and combine with 1 cup (250ml) water in a saucepan over medium heat. Gently simmer until the pears collapse and dissolve into the water. Purée the pears and set aside to cool.

Meanwhile, combine the remaining water with the sugar and bay leaves in a heavy-bottomed saucepan over medium heat. Bring to a boil, then simmer for 5 minutes. Remove the saucepan from the heat and leave to cool and infuse. Strain the syrup and discard the bay leaves.

Stir the syrup and lemon juice into the puréed pears and chill the mixture for at least 1 hour. Churn in an ice cream maker, according to the manufacturer's instructions. Serve immediately or transfer to a freezer container, cover the surface of the ice cream directly with waxed paper or foil and put in the freezer. Remove from the freezer 15 minutes before serving to allow it to soften slightly.

■ *This sorbet is delicious served with warm gingerbread, or on its own after a hearty, wintry meal.*

Geranium leaf sorbet
Fragrant

Scented geranium leaves give off a distinctive fragrance when passersby brush against them. This fragrance is captured in this delicate floral garden sorbet. Use organic geraniums – if you're unsure as to their origin, wash the leaves very well.

Makes 3 cups (750ml)

1 cup (200g) **extra-fine sugar**
1¼ cups (300ml) **water**
3–5 **scented geranium leaves**
2 Tbsp **lemon juice**
Extra geranium leaves for garnish

Combine the sugar, water and geranium leaves in a heavy-bottomed saucepan. Bring to a boil, reduce the heat and simmer for 5 minutes. Remove from the heat and allow to cool completely, to give the flavors time to infuse.

Strain the syrup into a 1-quart (1-liter) measuring jar and discard the leaves. Add water to reach 3 cups (750ml). The mixture should be sweet and full of flavor – add more water to taste if the flavor is too potent, because the leaves can be quite strong. Churn in an ice cream machine, according to the manufacturer's instructions, until frozen. Serve immediately or transfer to Popsicle molds and freeze. Before serving, adhere a leaf to the surface of the Popsicles with a dab of water. Return to the freezer for 10 minutes, then serve.

■ *Geranium leaves are available in many different scents, from lemon to rose – all make delicious sorbets.*

Geranium leaf sorbet

Pomegranate sorbet

Seductive

There is a geological thrill that comes from excavating the tiny rubylike seeds from pomegranates. Although this sorbet does require a lot of excavating, the glistening result is well worth the effort.

Makes 3 cups (700ml)

6 **pomegranates**
Scant ½ cup (75g) **extra-fine sugar**
1 Tbsp **corn syrup**
¼ cup (75ml) **water**
2 Tbsp **lemon juice**

Cut the pomegranates into quarters. Peel back the skin of each quarter and release the seeds into a bowl. Remove any bits of the bitter white membrane. Blend the seeds, then squeeze the pulp through fine cheesecloth into a bowl. Alternatively, push the pulp, a little at a time, through a fine sieve. This should yield 3 cups (700ml).

Meanwhile, combine the sugar, corn syrup and water in a small, heavy-bottomed saucepan. Bring to a boil, then simmer for 5 minutes.

Remove the saucepan from the heat and leave to cool.

Pour the cooled syrup into the pomegranate juice, then stir in the lemon juice. Cover and chill the mixture for 2 hours. Churn in an ice cream maker, according to the manufacturer's instructions, until frozen. Serve immediately or transfer to a freezer container, cover the surface directly with waxed paper or foil and put in the freezer.

■ *To serve pomegranate sorbet directly from the skins, cut 4 pomegranates in half, scoop out the seeds with a teaspoon and discard the bitter membranes. Place the bottom halves of skins in the freezer. Cut the remaining pomegranates as directed in the recipe. Spoon the frozen sorbet into the frozen skins.*

Pomegranate sorbet

Lemon curd ice cream

Zesty

This is a great ice cream to whip up for last-minute guests. You just need to allow enough time for freezing, but the actual preparation takes no time at all. This looks pretty served with candied lemon or lime peel if you have some on hand (see page 163).

Makes 2½ cups (600ml)

1¼ cups (300ml) **heavy cream**
1¼ cups (300ml) **lemon curd**
   bought or homemade (see page 165)

Whip the cream until soft peaks form. Add the lemon curd and continue beating until well combined. Transfer to a freezer container and still freeze (see page 17) for at least 6 hours.

■ *Variation: use lime, orange or grapefruit curd instead of the lemon curd for a change.*

■ *Serve scoops sandwiched inside small brioche or on top of toasted brioche or panettone slices.*

■ *Spoon some passionfruit pulp on top of the scoops – delicious!*

Lemon curd ice cream

Lemon and sage sorbet
Herbaceous

Lemon and sage sorbet makes a refreshing palate cleanser after an Italian meal of pasta and red wine.

Makes 3¼ cups (800ml)

2 cups (400g) **extra-fine sugar**
4 cups (900ml) **water**
12 **sage leaves**
Juice and zest of 3 **lemons**
   zest cut into long strips

Put the sugar, water, sage leaves and lemon zest strips into a saucepan and bring to a boil. Reduce the heat and simmer for 20 minutes. Cool the syrup overnight in the refrigerator, allowing the lemon and sage flavors to infuse. Remove the zest and sage leaves from the syrup. Strain the lemon juice and add to the syrup.

Churn in an ice cream maker, according to the manufacturer's instructions, for about 20 minutes, until frozen. Serve immediately or transfer to a freezer container, cover the surface with waxed paper or foil and put in the freezer.

Remove from the freezer 15 minutes before serving to allow to soften slightly.

■ *Put a couple of spoonfuls of Lemon and sage sorbet into a champagne flute or cocktail glass and top with vodka or limoncello (the Italian lemon-flavored liqueur) for a refreshing aperitif.*

Mango and basil granita

Icy

This granita is an interesting combination of mango and basil. Serve it in bowls with an extra scattering of shredded basil leaves.

Makes 3¼ cups (800ml)

3¾ cups (800g) **mango flesh**
½ cup (100g) **extra-fine sugar**
¼ cup (60ml) **water**
Juice of 1 **lemon**
6–8 **large basil leaves**
   chopped

Put all the ingredients in a food processor and process for 2–3 minutes or until smooth, scraping down the sides once or twice if necessary. Transfer the mixture to a freezer container and freeze, uncovered, for 1–2 hours or until crystals start to form.

Remove the granita from the freezer and, using a fork, vigorously break up all the ice crystals. Return to the freezer and repeat the process, breaking up the ice crystals, every 30 minutes for 2 hours. Return to the freezer to become firm. Remove the granita from the freezer 20 minutes before serving.

▧ *Variation: this is also delicious made with mint; just substitute 6–8 mint leaves for the basil.*

Rhubarb and ginger sorbet

Cleansing

Did you know that rhubarb is actually botanically classified as a vegetable? Make sure you remove any leaves before cooking, because they contain poisonous oxalic acid. The edible part is the crisp, pink stalk.

Makes 2½ cups (600ml)

1lb 3½oz (600g) **rhubarb** cut into 1-in (2-cm) pieces

Generous 1 cup (250g) **extra-fine sugar**

1¼ cups (300ml) **water**

1-in (2-cm) **gingerroot** peeled and finely grated

Juice of 1 **lemon**

Combine all the ingredients in a saucepan and bring to a boil. Cover and simmer until the rhubarb is tender, about 5 minutes. Leave to cool slightly before transferring to a food processor. Process until the mixture is combined but still has texture.

Churn in an ice cream maker, according to the manufacturer's instructions, until frozen. Transfer to a freezer container and cover the surface directly with waxed paper or foil. Freeze overnight.

Remove from the freezer 15 minutes before serving to allow it to soften slightly.

■ *Variation: rhubarb and cinnamon are also a great combination. Omit the ginger if you prefer or just add 2 teaspoons of cinnamon to it.*

■ *Make this sorbet when rhubarb is in season – the color will be pink and gorgeous.*

Rhubarb and ginger sorbet

Passionfruit sorbet

Fragrant

Leave the seeds of these fragrant and perfumed fruits in if you want a bit of crunch and texture, but if you prefer a smooth, pulp-free version, strain the syrup through a fine sieve before churning.

Makes 2½ cups (600ml)

20 **passionfruit**
   flesh scooped out
1¼ cups (600ml) **water**
1 cup (200g) **extra-fine sugar**
Juice of 2 **limes**

Place the passionfruit flesh, water, sugar and lime juice in a large saucepan. Stir until the sugar has dissolved. Bring to a boil, then reduce the heat and simmer for 5 minutes. Cool the syrup completely.

Churn in an ice cream maker, according to the manufacturer's instructions, until frozen. Serve immediately or transfer to a freezer container, cover the surface directly with waxed paper or foil and put in the freezer.

Remove from the freezer 15 minutes before serving to allow it to soften slightly.

■ *This is delicious served as part of a sorbet selection. Try it alongside Lemongrass sorbet (see page 70) and Raspberry and kaffir lime sorbet (see page 55).*

Passionfruit sorbet

Orange and poppy seed sorbet
Sweet

If you are worried about poppy seeds getting stuck in your teeth, then by all means leave them out. This refreshing orange sorbet is delicious on its own, particularly when served with crisp almond biscuits.

Makes 2½ cups (600ml)

1¼ cups (300ml) **freshly squeezed orange juice** strained
Juice of 1 **lemon**
1¼ cups (300ml) **water**
1½ cups (300g) **extra-fine sugar**
1 Tbsp **orange flower water (optional)**
1½ Tbsp **poppy seeds**

Combine all the ingredients except the poppy seeds in a saucepan and bring to a boil. Reduce the heat and simmer, uncovered, for 5 minutes. Allow the mixture to cool completely, then stir in the poppy seeds.

Churn in an ice cream maker, according to the manufacturer's instructions, for about 30 minutes or until frozen. Transfer to a freezer container, cover the surface directly with waxed paper or foil and put in the freezer.

Remove from the freezer 15 minutes before serving to allow it to soften slightly.

Variation: make this with blood oranges when they are in season for a vividly colored sorbet or add poppy seeds to your lemon sorbet if you prefer.

Kiwi fruit sorbet

Palate cleansing

Kiwi fruit, even when ripe, has a slightly acidic tang. When made into sorbet, we really get to appreciate the sweet quality of the fruit. Sometimes the color is a little paler than you would expect, but it tastes delicious nonetheless.

Makes 3 cups (750ml)

1lb (500g) **ripe kiwi fruit (about 8)**
¾ cup (150g) **extra-fine sugar**
1¼ cups (300ml) **water**
Juice of 1 **lemon**
2 **egg whites** (see note on page 4)
  lightly beaten with a fork

Put the kiwi fruit, sugar, water and lemon juice in a large saucepan and bring to a boil. Reduce the heat and simmer, uncovered, for 5 minutes or until the fruit is tender. Cool slightly then transfer to a food processor and process to a smooth purée. Allow to cool completely.

Churn in an ice cream maker, according to the manufacturer's instructions, for 10 minutes, then add the lightly beaten egg whites. Continue to churn until frozen, then serve immediately or transfer to a freezer container, cover the surface directly with waxed paper or foil and put in the freezer.

Remove from the freezer 15 minutes before serving to allow it to soften slightly.

■ *Golden kiwi fruit work just as well, too!*

Elderflower and violet frozen yogurt
Delicate

The essence of elderflower coupled with the sweet crunch of crystallized violets makes this an elegant Victorian-style ice. Crystallized violets can be bought in speciality food stores or made at home (see page 20).

Makes 1 quart (1L)

Scant 1 cup (200ml) **elderflower cordial**
½ cup (100ml) **water**
1¼ cups (300ml) **Greek yogurt**
1¼ cups (300ml) **crème fraîche or sour cream**
Juice of 1 **lemon**
½ cup (75g) **crystallized violets**

Combine the elderflower cordial and water in a small, heavy-bottomed saucepan and bring to a boil, stirring occasionally. Reduce the heat and simmer for 3–5 minutes, or until the liquid has reduced to a thin syrup. Remove from the heat and allow to cool.

Combine the yogurt and crème fraîche in a large bowl. Whisk in the syrup and lemon juice. Chill the mixture for 1 hour, then churn in an ice cream maker, according to the manufacturer's instructions.

Chop three quarters of the crystallized violets into smaller pieces, setting the remainder aside to decorate the finished ice. Just before the frozen yogurt has set (usually when 5 minutes remain), stir the chopped crystallized violets into the maker and continue to churn until set.

Serve immediately or transfer to a freezer container, cover the surface directly with waxed paper or foil and put in the freezer.

Decorate with the reserved crystallized violets to serve.

Elderflower and violet frozen yogurt

Lemon buttermilk sherbet

Tart

Buttermilk, despite its name, is a low-fat alternative to milk. It is slightly more sour in taste, but less cloying than milk, which lends a wonderful quality to ices. Unfortunately, the cream in this recipe cancels out the health properties of the buttermilk, but the union of the two is worth it!

Makes 4 cups (900ml)

1¼ cups (300ml) **fresh lemon juice** (approx. 5–7 lemons)
1½ cups (300g) **extra-fine sugar**
¾ cup (175ml) **buttermilk**
1¾ cups (400ml) **heavy cream**
½ cup (125ml) **corn syrup**
¼ tsp **salt**

Pour the lemon juice into a heavy-bottomed saucepan and heat over medium heat. Boil until it has reduced by half, about 15 minutes. Add the sugar and stir until dissolved. Remove from the heat and cool.

Stir the buttermilk, cream, corn syrup and salt into the lemon syrup, then chill for at least 2 hours. Churn in an ice cream maker, according to the manufacturer's instructions, then transfer to a freezer container, cover the surface directly with waxed paper or foil and freeze.

Decorate with citrus peel (see page 163) if desired.

If you are unable to find buttermilk, combine 1 tablespoon of lemon juice or white vinegar with 1 cup (250ml) milk. Allow to stand for 5 minutes and you will have something quite close to buttermilk.

Lemon buttermilk sherbet

Children's parties

It's a warm, sunny day. The freezer is filled with the fruits of your labor: Chocolate lamington ice cream, fruity frozen yogurt, Popsicles. The birds are singing and your garden is in full bloom. The scene is set for your child's birthday party.

Children's parties are all about fun and games, and ice cream always fits the bill. Forget the orderly table set with plates of ice cream and soggy cake. Action is what children want. Involvement. Creation. Mess. Scoop ice cream into cones and let them decorate the scoops with toppings or sprinkles. Sandwich ice cream between wafers and watch as they lap up the center and nibble the crusts. Serve colorful, multiflavored Popsicles. The layers will disappear, one by one. Spoon caramel brownie-studded ice cream into paper cups. The brownies become nuggets of gold awaiting excavation. Then, of course, for the *pièce de resistance*, nothing can beat a giant bowl – 12 scoops of ice cream, 12 toppings, a mountain of whipped cream and 12 little spoons. Guaranteed to be a hit every time.

Ice cream is fun. It's memory-making. It's messy. It makes a party.

or for the young at heart

Chocolate lamington ice cream
Coconutty

Lamingtons are a traditional New Zealand tea-time treat: plain sponge cake dipped in chocolate sauce and coated with coconut. Here, they are converted into vanilla ice cream with luscious swirls of chocolate and coconut sauce.

Makes 2½ cups (600ml)

⅔ cup (150ml) **Chocolate fudge sauce** (see page 164)
¼ cup (45g) **dry unsweetened coconut**
1¼ cups (300ml) **whole milk**
¾ cup (150g) **extra-fine sugar**
4 **large egg yolks**
Scant 1 cup (200ml) **heavy cream**

Combine the sauce and coconut in a small bowl and set aside.

Heat the milk in a saucepan to near-boiling point. In a heatproof bowl, beat the sugar and egg yolks, using an electric whisk, until thick and pale. Place over a saucepan of simmering water and stir in the milk. Stir occasionally until the mixture is thick enough to coat the back of a wooden spoon. Remove from the heat and cool completely.

When the mixture is cold, stir in the cream and churn in an ice cream maker, according to the manufacturer's instructions, for about 20 minutes, or until frozen. Spoon half of the ice cream into a freezer container. Add half of the chocolate-coconut sauce to the ice cream by spooning small amounts randomly over the surface. Top with the remaining ice cream and chocolate-coconut sauce. Use a blunt knife to drag the sauce through the ice cream 3–4 times to create a swirling effect. Cover the surface directly with waxed paper or foil and freeze overnight.

Chocolate lamington ice cream

Banana toffee ice cream

Creamy

You may be familiar with Banoffee pie – a banana, toffee and cream indulgence with a sprinkling of chocolate and a hint of coffee. Here is a child-friendly version, which omits the coffee and turns this popular pie into ice cream.

Makes 3 cups (750ml)

3½oz (100g) **peeled bananas**
Juice of 1 **lemon**
1¼ cups (100ml) **heavy cream**
1 tsp **vanilla extract**
⅔ cup (150ml) **sour cream**
1¾ cups (400ml) **canned sweetened condensed milk**
  caramelized (see page 20)
1oz (30g) **semisweet chocolate**
  grated (optional)

Purée the banana and lemon juice in a food processor until smooth. Whip the heavy cream with the vanilla extract until soft peaks form. Add the sour cream and caramelized condensed milk and continue whipping until well combined. Stir in the banana and chocolate, if using, and transfer to a freezer container. Cover the surface directly with waxed paper or foil and freeze overnight.

■ *Serve with an extra sprinkling of grated chocolate, if you like.*

Hokey pokey ice cream

Crunchy

This is as popular with adults as it is with children. Crunchy bits of honeycomb dispersed in vanilla ice cream – simple yet so good!

Makes 3¼ cups (800ml)

1 quantity **Vanilla ice cream** (see page 26)
   made to the custard stage, omitting the vanilla bean and
   using extra-fine sugar instead of vanilla sugar
5 Tbsp **granulated sugar**
2½ Tbsp **corn syrup**
1 tsp **baking soda**

Make the vanilla ice cream to the custard stage (when mixture coats the back of a wooden spoon) and, while the custard is cooling, make the hokey pokey. Dissolve the sugar and corn syrup in a heavy-bottomed saucepan over low heat, stirring constantly. Increase the heat and bring to a boil. Once boiling, reduce the heat and simmer for about 5 minutes or until the mixture is deep golden in color. Remove from the heat and stir in the baking soda. The mixture will bubble. Pour into a well-buttered shallow pan and allow to cool before smashing into pieces.

While the hokey pokey is cooling, continue with the ice cream. Add the cream to the custard and churn in an ice cream maker, according to the manufacturer's instructions, until frozen. Stir in the cooled, shattered hokey pokey and transfer to a freezer container. Cover the surface directly with waxed paper or foil and freeze.

Blueberry cheesecake ice cream

Blueberry cheesecake ice cream

Berrylicious

Cheesecakes were traditionally always baked. Nowadays they are also set with gelatin and refrigerated...and here is a frozen version to extend the cheesecake repertoire a little further.

Makes 2½ cups (600ml)

¾ cup (175ml) **whole milk**
3 **large egg yolks**
¾ cup (150g) **extra-fine sugar**
1¼ cups (300g) **cream cheese**
3½oz (100g) **white chocolate melted**
1 cup (250g) **Blueberry compôte** (see page 166)

Heat the milk gently to near-boiling point. In a separate, heatproof bowl, beat the egg yolks and sugar, using an electric whisk, until thick and pale. Place over a saucepan of simmering water and slowly add the milk, stirring constantly. Stir occasionally until the mixture is thick enough to coat the back of a wooden spoon. Remove from the heat and cool for 20 minutes.

Beat in the cream cheese, using an electric whisk, until smooth. Stir in the cooled, melted white chocolate and the blueberry compôte until just combined, then transfer to a freezer container. Cover the surface directly with waxed paper or foil and put in the freezer. After 1 hour, stir the mixture to prevent the berries from sinking to the bottom and return to the freezer for 4 hours or overnight. Serve with blueberry compôte drizzled over the top if desired.

■ *Variation: freeze in a foil-lined 7¾-in (20-cm) round cake pan. Once frozen, remove from the pan and slice into wedges.*

■ *Variation: use any homemade or store-bought berry or fruit compôte in place of the blueberry compôte.*

Traditional rocky road ice cream
Chunky

Rocky Road is like a treasure chest full of goodies...choose your favorite nuts, candy or broken cookies and make your own Rocky Road.

Makes 2½ cups (600ml)

1 quantity **Milk chocolate ice cream** (see page 30)
   using 5oz (150g) milk chocolate (instead of 3½oz (100g) milk chocolate) and 1¾oz (50g) bittersweet chocolate, unchurned
½ cup (60g) **whole almonds**
   toasted and chopped
½ cup (60g) **mini marshmallows**
½ cup (60g) **broken Graham crackers**
2oz (60g) **soft jelly candy**
   chopped if large

Churn the milk chocolate ice cream in an ice cream maker, according to the manufacturer's instructions, until almost frozen. Stir in the remaining ingredients and transfer to a freezer container with a lid or gently cover with waxed paper or foil and put in the freezer.

■ *Serve with Marshmallow sauce (see page 164) for complete indulgence.*

Traditional rocky road ice cream

Peppermint chocolate chip ice cream

Peppermint chocolate chip ice cream

Minty

Kids love the idea of green ice cream, and chocolate is always a bonus. It's fun to split the mixture in half and do half peppermint choc chip and half orange choc chip (see below).

Makes 2½ cups (600ml)

¼ cup (60g) **extra-fine sugar**
3 **large eggs**
  separated
1¼ cups (300ml) **whole milk**
5oz (150g) **white chocolate**
  broken into pieces
1½ tsp **peppermint extract**
1 tsp **green food coloring**
  (optional)
Scant 1 cup (200ml) **heavy cream**
¼ cup (45g) **chocolate chips, mini chocolate curls or mini chocolate buttons**

Beat the sugar and egg yolks in a heatproof bowl until thick and creamy. Place the bowl over a saucepan of simmering water and slowly add the milk, stirring occasionally until the mixture starts to thicken. When the mixture just begins to thicken, add the broken chocolate pieces, stirring continuously until the chocolate has melted and the mixture is smooth. Remove from the heat and stir in the peppermint extract and food coloring, if using. Cover the surface directly with plastic wrap and allow the mixture to cool completely.

When cold, stir in the cream and churn in an ice cream maker, according to the manufacturer's instructions, for about 20 minutes or until frozen. Stir in the chocolate chips and transfer to a freezer container. Cover the surface directly with waxed paper or foil and freeze.

■ *Variation: for orange chocolate chip ice cream, use the same quantity of orange extract and orange food coloring.*

■ *Children will probably prefer milk chocolate chips, but for adults it is best to add dark chocolate chips.*

Mango and yogurt slush

Mellow

This yogurt slush is a slightly healthier ice cream alternative that kids are bound to enjoy. It is creamy and easy to eat with a spoon.

Makes 3¼ cups (800ml)

2½ cups (600g) **fresh mango flesh**
1 cup (200g) **extra-fine sugar**
Scant 1 cup (200ml) **water**
Juice and grated zest of 2 **limes**
1¼ cups (300ml) **Greek yogurt**

Put the mango, sugar, water, lime juice and zest in a saucepan and bring to a boil. Reduce the heat and simmer, uncovered, for 5 minutes. Allow to cool for 10 minutes, then purée in a food processor or blender. Cool completely. Stir in the yogurt and and churn in an ice cream maker, according to the manufacturer's instructions until soft, slushy and almost frozen. Serve immediately.

■ *Variation: this can be transferred to a freezer container and frozen completely. Serve it in scoops if you choose to do this.*

Mango and yogurt slush

Vanilla and Rolo® brownie chunk

Heavenly

Here a caramel-studded brownie recipe is combined with the decadence of vanilla ice cream – a match made in heaven.

Makes 3¼ cups (800ml)

½ quantity **Rolo® brownies** (see page 167)
1 quantity **Vanilla ice cream** (see page 26)
   unchurned

Make the Rolo® brownies and freeze in bite-size pieces.

In an ice cream maker, churn the vanilla ice cream according to the manufacturer's instructions, until almost frozen. Stir in the brownie pieces. Transfer to a freezer container and cover the surface directly with waxed paper or foil and freeze for at least 3 hours.

■ *For extra indulgence, serve with a dollop of Caramel sauce (see page 165).*

■ *If you don't have time to make the brownies, simply stir in Rolos®, or your favorite chocolate bar chopped into bite-size pieces, into the vanilla ice cream.*

Milk chocolate chip cookie dough

Indulgent

This recipe is our take on a contemporary classic.

Makes 3 cups (700ml)

1 quantity **Milk chocolate ice cream** (see page 30)
   unchurned .
1¾ sticks (225g) **butter**
1¾ cups (250g) **light brown sugar**
Generous ½ cup (125g) **extra-fine sugar**
1 **large egg** (see note on page 4)
1 tsp **vanilla extract**
2½ cups (300g) **all-purpose flour**
1 tsp **baking soda**
¼ tsp **salt**
3½oz (100g) **semisweet** and 3½oz (100g) **milk chocolate**
   chopped or chocolate chips

Make the milk chocolate ice cream mixture, allow to cool completely, then refrigerate until required.

Beat the butter with both sugars. Add the egg and vanilla and beat until smooth. Sift in the flour, baking soda and salt. Add the chocolate and stir just until combined. Divide the dough in half – use one half for the ice cream. Roll it into teaspoon-sized balls and freeze. (Shape the other half into rounds and bake on parchment-lined baking sheets at 350°F (180°C) for 8 minutes until golden, or wrap well in plastic wrap and freeze.)

Transfer the ice cream mixture to the ice cream maker and churn according to the manufacturer's instructions. Just before the ice cream freezes, turn off the maker. Stir the frozen balls of cookie dough into the ice cream. Transfer to a freezer container, cover the surface directly with waxed paper or foil and freeze.

Peanut butter chocolate dip

Essential

The actor Bill Cosby once said "man cannot live by bread alone, he must have peanut butter." He certainly had a point, but how about about a little chocolate to go with that peanut butter? Chocolate and peanuts are a superb combination.

Makes 8 single-scoop ice cream cones

2¼ cups (500ml) **whole milk**
1 cup (250g) **smooth peanut butter**
¾ cup (150g) **extra-fine sugar**
2 tsp **vanilla extract**
5oz (150g) **semisweet chocolate**
¼ cup (30g) **peanuts**
  chopped
8 **ice cream cones**

Combine the milk, peanut butter and sugar in a heavy-bottomed saucepan over medium heat. Stir until smooth. Stir in the vanilla extract. Remove the saucepan from the heat and cool. Churn in an ice cream maker, according to the manufacturer's instructions. Spoon the ice cream into an airtight container and freeze for at least 2 hours.

Have a few large glasses (big enough to hold the cones upright) on hand. Melt the chocolate in a bowl over simmering water. Remove from the heat and cool slightly. Working quickly, scoop the ice cream onto the cones. Spoon the chocolate over the top, sprinkle with chopped nuts and place cones in the glasses. Freeze for 15 minutes, then enjoy!

Peanut butter chocolate dip

Grasshopper ice cream sandwiches

Grasshopper ice cream sandwiches
Decadent

The grasshopper, originally a cocktail made with crème de menthe and crème de cacao, has evolved into many green and chocolatey desserts. Here is its latest incarnation, this time as an ice cream sandwich.

Makes 6 sandwiches

12 **Double chocolate cookies** (see page 169)
6 **scoops Fresh mint ice cream** (see page 86)

Follow the recipe for the double chocolate cookies, making them as uniform as possible. Once baked, cool them and store in an airtight container.

Remove the ice cream from the freezer and let it stand for 15 minutes to soften. Line a baking sheet with baking parchment and place 6 cookies on it, bottom-sides up. Spoon a scoop of ice cream on to the cookies and sandwich with the remaining cookies, top-sides up. Gently press the cookies together to squash the ice cream in between. Smooth the edges with a knife. Serve immediately or cover the sheet with plastic wrap and return to the freezer.

■ *Variation: before serving, sprinkle the edge of the cookies with tiny colored candy.*

Watermelon and mint sorbet

Refreshing

A vibrant pink sorbet flecked with tiny bits of mint –
a perfectly sweet treat on a warm afternoon.

Makes 6¼ cups (1.5L)

½ cup (100g) **extra-fine
sugar**
⅔ cup (150ml) **water**
½ cup (30g) **mint leaves**
2lb 7oz (1.2kg) **watermelon
seeds removed and cut
into chunks**
Pinch of salt

Combine the sugar, water
and mint in a heavy-
bottomed saucepan. Bring
to a boil, then simmer for
5 minutes. Remove from the
heat and cool.

Strain the syrup and discard
the mint. Purée the
watermelon chunks until
smooth, then stir in the
cooled, strained syrup a little
at a time. The mixture should
be sweet, but this will vary
depending on the sweetness
of the water-melon. Add a
pinch of salt. Chill the mixture
for at least 1 hour, then
churn in an ice cream maker,
according to the
manufacturer's instructions.
Serve immediately or transfer
to a freezer container, cover
the surface directly with
waxed paper or foil and put
in the freezer.

Alternatively, pour the sorbet
mixture into Popsicle molds
and freeze.

Watermelon and mint sorbet

Popsicles

Popsicles

Playful

Once you've made your sugar syrup you can experiment with whatever fruit you have available. These ideas are just to get you started…

Makes 1¼ cups (300ml)

To make the sugar syrup:
1¾ cups (350g) **extra-fine sugar**
1½ cups (350ml) **water**

Put the sugar and water in a heavy-bottomed saucepan. Place over gentle heat until the sugar has dissolved, without boiling the mixture. Once the sugar has dissolved, increase the heat and bring to a boil. Boil the syrup for a further 5 minutes. Remove from the heat and cool before using.

Mixed berry and orange – put 1¾ cups (400g) frozen berries, ½ cup (100ml) sugar syrup, and the juice and grated zest of 1 orange in a food processor and process for 1–2 minutes or until liquefied. Strain through a fine sieve, then pour into Popsicle molds. Freeze.

Cantaloupe and lime – Put 1¾ cups (400g) of melon flesh, ½ cup (100ml) sugar syrup and the juice of 1 lime in a food processor and process for 1–2 minutes or until liquefied. Strain through a fine sieve, then pour into Popsicle molds. Freeze.

■ *To keep Popsicle sticks from floating to the top of your molds, soak them in warm water for an hour before inserting them into the molds.*

■ *Sugar syrup will last in the refrigerator for several weeks, so it's always a good idea to make up more than you need.*

Retro ices

The waiter in a soda fountain squirts hot fudge syrup into the bottom of a tall, narrow-footed glass. To this he adds two scoops of vanilla ice cream. He then pours in clear and bubbly soda, sending the ice cream bouncing to the surface. More hot fudge syrup is added, then a mound of whipped cream and a bright red cherry. He slides the ice cream soda down the counter into my ready and waiting hands. I'm at Sweet Sue's Tea Room and Soda Fountain in Bolingbroke, Georgia, one of the few authentic soda fountains left in America. Moments like these take most Americans, over the age of 60 that is, back to a time when life was as innocent as ice cream.

Ices have that magical ability. Perhaps it's because they symbolize sweeter times, leisure, vacation, comfort and rest – all moments worthy of revisiting. We have many treasured ice cream memories. For Pippa, Pistachio ice cream transports her to her days working in Italy, while a cool Saffron kulfi is reminiscent of travels in India. Pumpkin ice cream recreates Canadian Thanksgiving for me, and an icy sorbet takes me back to warm days in Provence.

Rum and raisin ice cream
Sophisticated

This ice cream is particularly creamy, and you can certainly taste the rum. Don't be tempted to tamper with this classic flavor – it's perfect as it is!

Makes 2½ cups (600ml)

¾ cup (100g) **raisins**
½ cup (100ml) **dark rum**
1¼ cups (300ml) **whole milk**
4 **large egg yolks**
¾ cup (100g) **soft brown sugar**
Scant 1 cup (200ml) **heavy cream**

Put the raisins and ¼ cup (75ml) of the rum in a small bowl and set aside to soak overnight or until the raisins have plumped up and absorbed almost all of the liquid.

Heat the milk in a heavy-bottomed saucepan to near-boiling point, then remove from the heat. Beat the egg yolks and sugar, using an electric whisk, in a heatproof bowl until thick and pale. Place over a saucepan of simmering water and stir in the milk. Stir occasionally until the mixture is thick enough to coat the back of a wooden spoon. Allow the mixture to cool completely.

When the mixture is cold, stir in the cream and the remaining rum. Churn in an ice cream maker, according to the manufacturer's instructions, until frozen. Stir in the raisins and transfer to a freezer container. Cover the surface directly with waxed paper or foil and freeze.

■ *Serve in Sugar and spice filo baskets (see page 171).*

Rum and raisin ice cream

Fruit mince ice cream
Festive

This is a great ice cream, made with ingredients from the pantry. If you have a jar of fruit mincemeat left over from Christmas, then try this for a post-holiday hit.

Makes 3¼ cups (800ml)

1 quantity **Vanilla ice cream** (see page 26)
    made to the custard stage, omitting the vanilla bean and
    using extra-fine sugar instead of vanilla sugar
1 tsp **vanilla extract**
⅔ cup (150g) **fruit mincemeat**
    bought or homemade

Make the Vanilla ice cream to the custard stage and allow the custard to cool completely.

When the custard is cool, add the heavy cream and vanilla extract and churn in an ice cream maker, according to the manufacturer's instructions, for about 20 minutes or until frozen. Stir in the mincemeat and transfer to a freezer container. Cover the surface directly with waxed paper or foil and freeze.

■ *A little grated orange or lemon zest will add further depth to the flavor.*

Saffron kulfi

Milky

Kulfi is the traditional ice cream of India, made by boiling milk until it reduces in volume. It is something of an acquired taste, a bit like evaporated milk and not particularly sweet. Traditional flavors for kulfi are usually pistachio, cardamom and rosewater, and on special occasions you will see it decorated with gold or silver leaf.

Makes 2½ cups (600ml)

2¼ cups (500ml) **whole milk**
1 cup (250ml) **heavy cream**
Pinch of saffron strands
2 Tbsp **honey**
½ tsp **orange flower water (optional)**

Put all the ingredients in a heavy-bottomed saucepan and bring to a boil. Reduce the heat and simmer until the mixture has reduced to 2¼ cups (500ml), about 30 minutes, stirring occasionally. Cool completely, then churn in an ice cream maker, according to the manufacturer's instructions, until frozen.

Transfer to individual conical molds or one large freezer container. Cover the surfaces directly with waxed paper or foil. To serve, remove the cones from the freezer about 30 minutes before serving. They should then tip easily out of the molds.

■ *Serve with chopped pistachios or slivered almonds.*

■ *If you have trouble removing the molds, try dipping them briefly in hot water. This should soften the ice cream slightly so that you can ease it out.*

Pistachio ice cream

Subtle

This ice cream is the ultimate in sophistication. An almost savory–sweet finish to a meal, which is perfectly complemented by a glass of vin santo or other sweet dessert wine.

Makes 3 cups (750ml)

3½oz (100g) **shelled pistachios**
1¾ cups (400ml) **whole milk**
4 **large egg yolks**
¾ cup (150g) **extra-fine sugar**
Scant 1 cup (200ml) **heavy cream**

Grind the pistachios to a fine powder using a food processor or coffee grinder. Take care not to overprocess.

Put the ground nuts and milk in a saucepan and bring to near-boiling point. Remove from the heat and strain through a fine sieve or cheesecloth. Beat the eggs and sugar, using an electric whisk, in a heatproof bowl, until thick and pale. Place over a saucepan of simmering water and slowly stir in the milk. Stir occasionally until the mixture is thick enough to coat the back of a wooden spoon. Allow the mixture to cool.

Stir in the cream and churn in an ice cream maker, according to the manufacturer's instructions, until frozen. Serve immediately or transfer to a freezer container, cover the surface with waxed paper or foil and put in the freezer.

■ *Serve with an extra sprinkling of pistachios.*

Licorice and star anise swirl ice cream

Aniseed

Not everyone likes the aniseed flavor of licorice and star anise, but if you are a fan then you'll love this double hit all in one. This one's for my good friend Sez, who has a passion for anything licorice.

Makes 3¼ cups (800ml)

3½oz (100g) **soft licorice** coarsely chopped
3 Tbsp (30ml) **boiling water**
1½ cups (350ml) **whole milk**
3 **star anise**
4 **large egg yolks**
¾ cup (100g) **soft brown sugar**
1 cup (250ml) **heavy cream**

Put the licorice and boiling water in a food processor and process to form a paste. Set aside.

Put the milk and star anise in a small saucepan and bring to near-boiling point. Turn off the heat and allow the milk to infuse for 20–30 minutes. Using an electric whisk, beat the egg yolks and sugar in a heatproof bowl until thick and pale. Place over a pan of simmering water and slowly stir in the infused milk. Stir occasionally until the mixture is thick enough to coat the back of a wooden spoon. Add the licorice paste and continue stirring for a further 2–3 minutes. Remove from the heat and allow the mixture to cool completely.

Add the heavy cream to the cooled mixture and churn in an ice cream maker, according to the manufacturer's instructions, until frozen, then serve or transfer to a freezer container and put in the freezer. Alternatively, whip the cream until soft peaks form and fold thoroughly into the cooled custard. Transfer to a freezer container, cover with waxed paper or foil, and freeze.

Green tea and ginger parfait

Enchanting

This light and fluffy parfait is subtly infused with green tea and ginger. It's an interesting combination and well worth a try.

Makes 2½ cups (600ml)

1¾ cups (400ml) **whole milk**
3 **green tea bags**
1-in (2-cm) **piece gingerroot**
  coarsely chopped
4 **large eggs** (see note on page 4)
  separated
½ cup (100g) **extra-fine sugar**
Scant 1 cup (200ml) **heavy cream**

Put the milk, tea bags and ginger in a medium saucepan and bring to near-boiling point. Remove from the heat and cool for 30 minutes, allowing the flavor to infuse the milk.

Using an electric whisk, beat the egg yolks and sugar in a heatproof bowl until thick and pale. Place over a saucepan of simmering water and stir in the still-warm strained milk. Stir occasionally until the mixture is thick enough to coat the back of a wooden spoon. Cool completely. When the custard mixture is cold, gently beat the egg whites and cream, in separate bowls, until soft peaks form. Fold the cream, then the egg whites gently into the custard mixture and transfer to a freezer container. Cover the surface directly with waxed paper or foil and freeze overnight.

▓ *Variation: you could try this using another type of your favorite tea, perhaps Earl Grey or peppermint tea. Infuse the milk in exactly the same way.*

Green tea and ginger parfait

Ginger snap ice cream

Festive

This is a must for ginger lovers, intense and irresistible.

Makes 2½ cups (600ml)

½ quantity **Brandy snap baskets** (see page 168)
Scant 1 cup (200ml) **water**
¼ cup (75ml) **corn syrup**
½ cup (75g) **light brown sugar**
1 Tbsp **ground ginger**
1¼ cups (300ml) **heavy cream**
¼ cup (75g) **preserved ginger**
   chopped (optional)

Prepare the brandy snaps, without shaping them into baskets, and set aside to cool. Once cool, shatter the snaps into small pieces.

Combine the water, golden syrup, sugar and ground ginger in a medium saucepan and stir until the sugar has dissolved. Simmer the mixture, uncovered, for 5 minutes. Cool completely.

Using an electric whisk, whip the cream in a large bowl until stiff peaks form. Stir in the cooled ginger syrup and continue beating for a further 30 seconds or until well combined. Stir in the broken brandy snaps and preserved ginger, if using. Pour into a freezer container, cover the surface directly with waxed paper or foil and freeze.

■ *Variation: buy readymade brandy snaps instead of making them if you are short of time. Alternatively, you can leave out the brandy snaps altogether for a ginger ice cream without the crunch.*

Banana, nutmeg and soy milk ice cream
Soothing

Here is the perfect ice cream for those of you who have a lactose intolerance, although it can be enjoyed by anyone. Just remember that soy milk has rather a different taste to cow's milk, so expect something different.

Makes 2½ cups (600ml)

7oz (200g) **bananas (peeled weight)**
   chopped
⅔ cup (150ml) **water**
½ cup (100g) **extra-fine sugar**
2 tsp **ground nutmeg**
¼ cup (45ml) **honey**
1 cup (250ml) **soy milk**
2 **large egg yolks**
Scant ½ cup (75g) **extra-fine sugar**

Put the chopped banana, water, sugar, nutmeg and honey in a saucepan and bring to a boil. Reduce the heat and simmer, uncovered, for 5 minutes. Cool slightly, then place in a food processor and process to a purée.

Heat the soy milk in a heavy-bottomed saucepan to near-boiling point. Using an electric whisk, beat the egg yolks and sugar in a heatproof bowl until thick and pale. Place over a saucepan of simmering water and stir in the soy milk. Stir occasionally until the mixture is thick enough to coat the back of a wooden spoon. Allow to cool completely before combining with the banana purée. Churn in an ice cream maker, according to the manufacturer's instructions. Serve immediately or transfer to a freezer container, cover the surface of the ice cream directly with waxed paper or foil and put in the freezer.

Virgin mojito
Refreshing

The Cuban Mojito cocktail, which is made with rum, sugar, lime, mint and soda water, captures the essence of summer. Add a few spoonfuls of this mint and lime sorbet to a glass and top it up with white rum and soda, then you end up with both the drink and the sorbet – what more could you want!

Makes 3¼ cups (800ml)

2¼ cups (400g) **raw sugar**
4 cups (900ml) **water**
½ cup (30g) **fresh mint leaves, plus extra to decorate**
Zest and juice of 4 **limes**
   zest cut into long strips

Put the sugar, water, mint and lime zest strips into a saucepan and bring to a boil. Reduce the heat and simmer for 20 minutes. Cool the syrup overnight in the refrigerator, allowing the lime and mint to infuse.

Remove the zest and mint from the syrup before adding the strained lime juice. Churn in an ice cream maker, according to the manufacturer's instructions, for 20 minutes or until frozen. Serve immediately or transfer to a freezer container, cover the surface directly with waxed paper or foil and put in the freezer. Before serving, allow the sorbet to soften slightly to regain its slushy texture. Decorate with extra mint leaves.

Virgin mojito

Vanilla, caramel and pecan ice cream

Scrumptious

Sometimes a little salt with your dessert adds a surprising, yet welcome tang.

Makes 1 quart (1L)

1 quantity **Salty-sweet pecans** (see page 162)
1 quantity **Caramel sauce** (see page 165)
1 quantity **Vanilla ice cream** (see page 26)
   unchurned

Make the salty-sweet pecans and caramel sauce and allow to cool. In an ice cream maker, churn the vanilla ice cream, according to the manufacturer's instructions, stopping just before the ice cream has set.

Stir the pecans into the partly-set vanilla ice cream. Spoon half the ice cream into an airtight container. Cover with swirls of caramel sauce, then spoon the remaining ice cream over the top. Top with more caramel swirls. Using a blunt knife, cut through the layers and swirl the sauce through the ice cream. Any remaining sauce can be stored in an airtight container in the refrigerator for up to 2 weeks. Transfer to a freezer container, cover the surface directly with waxed paper or foil and put in the freezer for at least 30 minutes.

■ *Almonds or walnuts can be substituted for the pecans.*

Chocolate peanut butter wave

Luscious

Cousin Claire always has a chocolate and peanut butter birthday cake. In fact, she had a chocolate and peanut butter wedding cake, too. This one is for her.

Makes 3 cups (700ml)

1 quantity **Milk chocolate ice cream** (see page 30) churned until almost set

For the peanut butter chunks:
½ cup (125g) **crunchy peanut butter**
2 Tbsp **butter**
   softened
2oz (60g) **confectioner's sugar**
4 Tbsp **Rice Krispies®**

To make the peanut butter chunks, combine the peanut butter, butter and confectioner's sugar. Mix well. Stir in the Rice Krispies® and gently mix until incorporated.

When the chocolate ice cream has almost set, stir in ½ teaspoon-size balls of the peanut butter mixture. Stir until combined. Transfer to a freezer container, cover the surface directly with waxed paper or foil and put in the freezer.

■ *For the ultimate in decadence, serve with a dollop of chocolate sauce on top.*

Pumpkin ice cream
Cool warmth

Pumpkin pie is the traditional Thanksgiving dessert, and this ice cream captures the distinctive, comforting flavors of nutmeg and cinnamon in one, cool package.

Makes 1 quart (1L)

1¾ cups (400ml) **whole milk**
3 **large egg yolks**
1 cup (200g) **extra-fine sugar**
1 15-oz (450-g) **can pumpkin purée**
½ tsp **nutmeg**
¼ tsp **cinnamon**
1 cup (250ml) **heavy cream**
1 tsp **vanilla extract**

Heat the milk in a heavy-bottomed saucepan to near-boiling point. In a separate, heatproof bowl, beat the eggs with the sugar, using an electric whisk, until thick and pale. Gradually stir the milk into the egg mixture. Place the bowl over a saucepan of simmering water and continue stirring until the mixture is thick enough to coat the back of a wooden spoon. Remove the bowl from the heat and allow to cool.

When cool, whisk in all of the remaining ingredients and cover the surface directly with plastic wrap or waxed paper to prevent a skin from forming. Place in the refrigerator and chill for at least 1 hour.

Churn in an ice cream maker, according to the manufacturer's instructions. Serve immediately or transfer to a freezer container, cover the surface directly with waxed paper or foil and put in the freezer.

Pumpkin ice cream

Southern iced tea sorbet

Refreshing

Iced tea is a popular summer drink and is equally delicious and refreshing made into a cooling sorbet and served in a tall glass. Serve with lots of fresh mint to decorate, and, of course, enjoy it slowly, as they would in the Deep South.

Makes 1 quart (1L)

8 **tea bags**
½ cup (90g) **fresh mint leaves,** plus extra to decorate
5½ cups (1.25L) **boiling water**
¾ cup (175g) **extra-fine sugar**
⅔ cup (175ml) **freshly squeezed lemon juice**

Place the tea bags and mint in a large teapot or jar, cover with the boiling water and leave to infuse for 30 minutes.

Strain the liquid into a bowl. Add the sugar and lemon juice and taste. The mixture should be sweet, lemony, with a hint of mint. If it's too tart, add more sugar, and if it's too sweet, more lemon juice. Strain the mixture again to remove any lemon pulp or mint, and chill for 1 hour.

Churn in an ice cream maker, according to the manufacturer's instructions. Sorbets are best scooped out of the machine, but if you are making this in advance, spoon it into an airtight container, cover the surface directly with baking parchment and put in the freezer. Before serving, let the frozen sorbet soften slightly so it regains its slushy texture. Decorate with fresh mint.

Chocolate and coconut banana split

Indulgent

You can't beat a banana split. What more can we say?

Makes 4

½ cup (125ml) **heavy cream**
4 **bananas**
   peeled and split
   lengthwise
4 scoops **Milk chocolate
   ice cream** (see page 30)
4 scoops **Dark chocolate
   ice cream** (see page 33)
4 scoops **Coconut ice
   cream** (see page 83)
½ cup (125ml) **Chocolate
   fudge sauce**
   (see page 164)
4–6 Tbsp **toasted dry
   unsweetened coconut,
   to taste** (see page 20)

Have four banana split dishes at the ready. In a metal bowl, whip the cream until soft peaks form. Place two banana halves in each dish. Spoon one scoop of each ice cream in between the bananas. Drizzle chocolate fudge sauce over the ice cream. Top with whipped cream and a sprinkling of toasted coconut. (See page 141 for photograph.)

■ *Use any combination of ice creams, sauces and toasted nuts for this recipe.*

Vanilla and ginger beer ice cream soda

Reminiscent

The ice cream floats, the ginger beer becomes creamy – it's bubbly indulgence at its best.

Serves 4

1 quantity **Vanilla ice cream** (see page 26)
1 quart (1L) **ginger beer or root beer**

Spoon the ice cream into four tall glasses. Top with ginger or root beer. Insert bendy straws, stir and enjoy!

Strawberry fizz

Indulgent

Summertime in a glass.

Serves 4

½ cup (125ml) **Mixed berry coulis** (see page 171)
1 quantity **Strawberry ice cream** (see page 29)
Soda water

You'll need four tall glasses. Put a few spoonfuls of coulis into the bottom of each glass. Spoon two scoops of ice cream on top, and top with more coulis. Fill the glasses with soda water, insert straws and enjoy! (See page 140 for photograph.)

Vanilla and ginger beer ice cream soda

Accompaniments

Salty-sweet pecans

Thanks to our friend and food writer, Nina Simonds, for this addictive recipe.

Makes 2 cups (250g)

1 large egg white
  lightly beaten
2 cups (250g) **pecan nuts**
¼ cup (60g) **extra-fine sugar**
1½ tsp **Chinese five-spice powder**
1 tsp **salt**

Preheat the oven to 325°F (160°C). Lightly grease a baking sheet with oil, or cover with baking parchment.

Combine the beaten egg white with the pecans and stir to coat. In a paper or a plastic bag, mix the sugar with the Chinese five-spice powder. Drain the pecans in a strainer and drop them into the bag. Holding the bag shut, shake it to coat the pecans with the sugar and spice mixture. Spread the coated nuts in a single layer on the baking sheet and roast, stirring occasionally, for 35–40 minutes until golden and crisp. To check if they are done, cut a pecan in half and make certain the inside is crisp. Allow to cool.

These will keep for up to 1 week in an airtight container and for 2–3 months in the freezer.

◼ *To re-crisp the nuts, bake them in the oven at 350°F (180°F) until crisp.*

Candied citrus peel

Try to use unwaxed, preferably organic citrus fruits. If this is not possible, wash fruit thoroughly.

4–6 **mixed citrus fruits**
    (grapefruit, oranges, lemons, limes)
1½ cups (300g) **extra-fine sugar**
Scant 1 cup (200ml) **water**

Using a wide, horizontal vegetable peeler, peel the skin from the fruit, making sure not to peel away the bitter white pith. Finely slice the peel into matchsticks. Set aside.

Combine 1 cup (200g) of the sugar with the water in a heavy-bottomed sauce-pan and bring to a boil. Boil the mixture gently until the sugar dissolves. Add the chopped peel, reduce the heat and simmer gently for 30 minutes. Remove the peel with a slotted spoon and place, separated, on to a plate.

Place the remaining sugar in a bowl. Toss the cooled peel in the sugar, then leave to dry on a clean cloth. Store in an airtight container; it will keep for several months.

Marshmallow sauce

Makes 1 cup (250ml)

⅓ cup (90ml) **corn syrup**
¼ cup (60g) **extra-fine sugar**
1 **large egg white** (see note on page 4)

Combine the syrup with 1 tablespoon of water in a small saucepan. Bring to a boil, brushing the sides of the pan with a wet pastry brush to keep the syrup from crystallizing.

In a medium bowl, beat the egg white until stiff. When the syrup reaches 250°F (120°C) after about 7 minutes, slowly pour the syrup down the side of the bowl, beating well until the mixture is shiny and fluffy. Use immediately, or store in an airtight container in the refrigerator for up to 1 week (it may need a stir before serving).

This sauce remains gooey when chilled or frozen.

Chocolate fudge sauce

Makes 1½ cups (350ml)

½ cup (75g) **soft brown sugar**
½ stick (45g) **butter**
½ cup (125ml) **corn syrup**
1 Tbsp **unsweetened cocoa**
⅔ cup (150ml) **heavy cream**
2oz (60g) **semisweet chocolate**
½ tsp **vanilla extract**

Combine the sugar, butter, corn syrup and cocoa in a saucepan over very low heat until the sugar has dissolved. Bring to a gentle boil and cook, uncovered, for 5 minutes. Remove the saucepan from the heat and stir in the cream, chocolate and vanilla extract. Stir well until the chocolate has melted. Return to the heat and cook for a further 1 minute or until smooth.

Serve the sauce hot over ice cream or allow to cool and swirl through ice cream.

This sauce will keep for up to 2 weeks in an airtight container in the refrigerator.

Caramel sauce

Makes 2½ cups (600ml)

2 cups (400g) **extra-fine sugar**
½ cup (125ml) **water**
1½ cups (350ml) **heavy cream**
2 Tbsp **sweet butter**
1 tsp **vanilla extract**
1 tsp **lemon juice**

Combine the sugar and water in a heavy-bottomed saucepan over medium heat. Stir until the sugar dissolves, then stop stirring and bring the syrup to a boil. Brush the sides of the saucepan with a wet pastry brush to keep the sugar from crystallizing on the side of the saucepan. Swirl the saucepan as the syrup begins to brown. When the syrup is a dark amber color—approximately 350°F (180°C) on a sugar thermometer (watch carefully, the syrup can easily burn)—reduce the heat to low and add the cream. Stir as the syrup bubbles and splatters until smooth. Add the butter and vanilla and stir until the butter melts. Finish the sauce with a squirt of lemon juice.

Allow the sauce to cool before using it in an ice cream recipe or storing it in the refrigerator. It will keep for 2 weeks in an airtight container in the refrigerator.

Lemon curd

Makes 1¾ cups (400ml)

1 stick (100g) **sweet butter**
¾ cup (150g) **extra-fine sugar**
Finely grated zest and juice of 3 **lemons**
3 **large eggs**
  beaten

Put the butter, sugar, lemon zest and juice in a heatproof bowl. Place over a saucepan of simmering water and stir over low heat until the sugar has dissolved and the mixture is warm. Whisk the warm lemon mixture into the beaten eggs and strain through a nonmetallic sieve. Return the mixture to the heatproof bowl and place over the still simmering water. Stir occasionally until the mixture thickens and coats the back of a wooden spoon. Do not allow the mixture to boil or it will curdle.

Pour the hot mixture into hot, sterilized jars and seal well. The lemon curd will keep for up to 1 month if stored in a cool place.

Blueberry compôte

Makes 1¼ cups (300ml)

Juice of 1 **orange**
1 tsp **cornstarch**
1 cup (200g) **fresh blueberries**
2 Tbsp **extra-fine sugar**

Combine the orange juice and cornstarch in a small bowl. Put the blueberries, sugar and cornstarch mixture in a small saucepan over low heat. Stir gently until the blueberries begin to macerate and their juice just starts to run. Stir gently for a further 30 seconds, then remove from the heat and allow to cool. Store in the refrigerator for up to 1 week.

Winter fruits and ginger compôte

Makes 3 cups (800ml)

2½ cups (600ml) **water**
Generous 1 cup (250g) **extra-fine sugar**
1 **cinnamon stick**
Zest and juice of 1 **orange**
   zest cut in long strips
Scant ¼ cup (45g) **preserved ginger**
   cut into strips
12 **dried apricots**
12 **prunes**
   pitted
2 **pears**
   peeled, cored and cut into quarters
2 **apples**
   peeled, cored and cut into quarters

Bring the water, sugar, cinnamon, orange zest and juice to a boil. Reduce the heat and simmer for 10 minutes. Add the remaining ingredients and poach until the fruit is tender, about a further 15 minutes. Allow the fruits to cool in the syrup. Serve cold over ice cream or other desserts. Store in the refrigerator for up to 1 week.

Rolo® brownies

Makes 96 bite-size pieces

1 cup (115g) **Rolos®**
5 oz (150g) **bittersweet chocolate (70% cocoa solids)**
1 stick (100g) **butter**
  cubed
1 cup (200g) **extra-fine sugar**
1 tsp **vanilla extract**
2 **large eggs**
1 cup (125g) **all-purpose flour**
¼ tsp **baking powder**
¼ tsp **salt**

Preheat the oven to 350°F (180°C). Line a 8 x 8-in (20 x 20-cm) pan with foil, leaving extra foil to overhang the sides of the pan.

Cut the Rolos® in half and set aside.

Melt the chocolate and butter in a heatproof bowl set over a saucepan of simmering water, stirring occasionally. Remove from the heat and allow to cool.

When cool, whisk in the sugar and vanilla extract. Whisk in the eggs, one at a time, until the mixture is shiny. Sift the flour, baking powder and salt into the chocolate mixture and stir to combine. Spoon the mixture into the prepared pan. Place the Rolo® halves over the top, bearing in mind that the cooked brownies will be cut into bite-size pieces, so the closer the Rolos®, the better.

Bake the brownies for 35 minutes, or until just set in the middle. Using the overhanging foil as handles, lift the brownies out of the pan and leave to cool on a wire rack. When completely cool, cut the brownies into bite-size pieces and freeze the pieces for up to 2 months in an airtight container.

Brandy snap baskets

Makes 8

½ stick (60g) **sweet butter**
¼ cup (60g) **extra-fine sugar**
¼ cup (60ml) **corn syrup**
1 tsp **ground ginger**
1 tsp **vanilla extract**
1 Tbsp **brandy**
Grated zest of 1 **lemon**
½ cup (60g) **all-purpose flour**

Put the butter, extra-fine sugar and corn syrup in a medium saucepan and heat, stirring regularly, until the butter and corn syrup have melted. Leave to simmer for a further 2 minutes, then remove from the heat. Stir in the ginger, vanilla extract, brandy and lemon zest. Gradually add the flour and mix until all the ingredients are well incorporated. Set the mixture aside for 10–15 minutes to allow it to cool and become firmer.

Preheat the oven to 375°F (190°C). Place large spoonfuls of the mixture on a nonstick or well-greased baking sheet. Allow plenty of room between each – you may want to cook them in two batches of four. Cook for 10–12 minutes or until the brandy snaps are well spread and rich golden brown. Remove them from the oven and allow to cool for 1 minute. Place the slightly cooled snaps (they should still be pliable) over upside-down dariole molds or small ramekins. Set these aside until they cool and harden.

Store your brandy snap baskets in an airtight container until ready to use. They will keep for up to 1 month.

Double chocolate cookies

Makes 30 cookies

2 sticks (200g) **butter**
Generous 1 cup (250g) **extra-fine sugar**
¾ cup (125g) **brown sugar**
1 **large egg**
1 tsp **vanilla extract**
¼ cup (45g) **unsweetened cocoa**
2 Tbsp **whole milk**
2 cups (250g) **all-purpose flour**
¾ tsp **baking soda**
5oz (150g) **chopped semisweet chocolate**

Preheat the oven to 350°F (180°C). In a large mixing bowl, cream the butter and sugars. Beat in the egg and vanilla extract, then the cocoa and milk. Sift in the flour and baking soda until just blended. Stir in the chopped chocolate.

Line a baking sheet with baking parchment. Shape the dough into uniform tablespoon-size balls and place on the sheet, 2in (5cm) apart. Bake for 12 minutes, leave to cool on the sheet for a few minutes, then transfer to a wire rack to cool completely. Store the cookies in an airtight container. Eat within 2 weeks.

Candied kumquats

Thanks to our friend and food writer, Pam Shookman, for this recipe.

Makes 5 cups (1kg)

2½ cups (500ml) **orange juice**
2 cups (400g) **extra-fine sugar**
5 cups (1kg) **kumquats**

Bring the orange juice and sugar to a boil in a large, heavy-bottomed saucepan, stirring to dissolve the sugar. Add the kumquats and bring the mixture back to a boil.

Cut a dampened piece of baking parchment to fit the circumference of the saucepan and place it directly on the surface of the syrup. (This will keep the syrup from thickening before the kumquats have cooked.) Simmer until the syrup is thick and the kumquats have collapsed and appear slightly translucent. Store the kumquats in the syrup in the refrigerator or seal in airtight jars. They will keep in the refrigerator for up to 2 months.

Easy maple syrup cones

Makes 12 cones

6 **round soft tortillas**
   about 8in (20cm) in diameter
¼ cup (45ml) **maple syrup**
½ stick (45g) **butter**
½ cup (60g) **raw sugar**

Preheat the oven to 350°F (180°C).

Cut each tortilla into half and set aside. Melt the maple syrup and butter in a small saucepan. Remove from the heat and stir in the sugar, but do not allow the sugar to dissolve completely.

Brush one tortilla half on both sides with the sugar mixture. Place the pointed end of a metal cone in the center of the flat tortilla edge. Wrap the tortilla around the cone and secure the end with half a cocktail stick. Leave the tortilla on the metal cone to cook. If you do not have 12 metal cones, you may have to do this in batches. Repeat the process until all the tortilla halves have been used.

Bake in the preheated oven for 5 minutes. Baste each cone with more syrup and cook for a further 5 minutes or until golden and crisp. Allow the cones to cool slightly before removing the metal cone. Set aside to cool completely before serving.

Mixed berry coulis

Makes 1¼ cups (300ml)

¼ cup (60ml) **cassis**
1 cup (200g) **mixed berries of choice**
   (raspberries, blackberries, blueberries)
1 cup (200g) **extra-fine sugar**
Scant 1 cup (200ml) **water**

Heat the cassis, berries, sugar and water in a medium saucepan and bring to a boil. Reduce the heat and simmer for 10 minutes. Transfer the berry mix to a food processor and whiz to a purée. Pass the purée through a sieve to remove any seeds. Return to the pan and simmer for a further 10–15 minutes or until the mixture thickens in consistency. Allow to cool and serve poured over ice cream.

Sugar and spice phyllo baskets and wafers

Makes 24 small/12 large wafers or 6 baskets

1 stick (100g) **sweet butter**
2 tsp **ground cinnamon or mixed spice**
3 Tbsp **soft brown sugar**
8 sheets **phyllo pastry**
¾ cup (100g) **ground almonds**

Preheat the oven to 350°F (180°C). Put the butter, cinnamon and sugar in a small saucepan and melt.

Arrange one sheet of phyllo on a clean counter and brush the melted butter mixture evenly over the pastry surface. Sprinkle with an eighth of the ground almonds. Place another sheet of phyllo on top and repeat the procedure until you have four layered sheets, finishing with ground almonds. Cut the stack into 12 even squares and place on a baking sheet. Alternatively, cut into six larger squares and shape over small ramekins to form a basket shape when cooked.

Repeat with the remaining phyllo, butter mix and almonds. Bake for 8–10 minutes until the pastry is golden and crisp. Cool before serving.

Lemon and hazelnut biscotti

Makes 24-32

2¼ cups (275g) **all-purpose flour**
¾ cup (150g) **extra-fine sugar**
1 tsp **baking powder**
2 **large eggs plus 1 egg yolk**
Grated zest of 1 **lemon**
1 cup (100g) **whole hazelnuts**
  blanched

Preheat the oven to 350°F (180°C).

Put the flour, extra-fine sugar and baking powder in a large bowl and mix together. In a separate bowl, beat the eggs, egg yolk and lemon zest until just combined. Add to the dry ingredients and mix together. Add the hazelnuts and use your hands to combine all the ingredients thoroughly. Transfer to a clean surface and knead for a couple of minutes.

Divide the mixture into four balls and shape each ball into a long, flattened cigar shape. Put on a baking sheet lined with baking parchment and bake for 20 minutes. Remove from the oven and cut each long cookie into six to eight pieces. Lay the cookies flat on the tray and return to the oven for a further 10 minutes or until golden. Leave to cool before serving. Biscotti can be stored in an airtight container for up to 1 month.

Crispy almond and lemon triangles

Makes 20

1 Tbsp **all-purpose flour**
1 Tbsp **ground almonds**
¼ cup (45g) **extra-fine sugar**
Grated zest of 1 **lemon**
1 **egg white**
  lightly beaten
½ tsp **vanilla extract**
2 Tbsp **melted butter**
⅕ cup (30g) **slivered almonds**

Preheat the oven to 350°F (180°C).

Line the base of a baking pan, 9 x 13in (30 x 25cm), with baking parchment. Sift the flour, ground almonds and extra-fine sugar into a small bowl. Stir in the lemon zest, egg white, vanilla extract and melted butter. Pour the mixture into the prepared pan and spread evenly to cover the surface. Sprinkle over the slivered almonds. Bake for 12–14 minutes or until firm when pressed lightly and golden brown.

Remove from the oven. Transfer the baking parchment on to a cutting board and trim the edges of the cookie. Cut the cookie in half lengthwise, then cut each half into ten triangles. Allow to cool before serving with your favorite ice cream.

Variation: omit the lemon zest and ground almonds and add 1 tablespoon unsweetened cocoa to the mixture to make Crispy chocolate almond triangles.

Bibliography

Beer, Maggie; *Maggie's Table* (Viking, 2001)

Cohen, Ben and Greenfeld, Jerry; *Ben & Jerry's Ice Cream and Dessert Book* (Workman Publishing NY, 1987)

Crawford Poole, Shona; *Ice Cream and Other Desserts* (Conran Octopus, 2001)

Davidson, Alan; *The Oxford Companion to Food* (Oxford University Press, 1999)

Durack, Terry; *Yum* (New Holland, 1998)

Grimes, LuLu and Halsey, Kay; *Food – The Definitive Guide* (Murdoch Books, 2002)

Hazan, Marcella; *Marcella's Kitchen* (MacMillan, 1986)

Lawson, Nigella; *How to Eat* (Chatto & Windus, 1998)

Lidell, Caroline and Weir, Robin; *Ices – The Definitive Guide* (Grub Street, 1998)

McGee, Harold; *On Food and Cooking* (Fireside, 1984)

Robuchon, Joel; *Larousse Gastronomique* (Paul Hamlyn, 1997)

Rogers, Judy; *The Zuni Café Cookbook* (W.W. Norton and Company, 2002)

Roux, Michel; *Sauces* (Quadrille Publishing, 2002)

Stewart, Martha; *The Martha Stewart Cookbook* (Clarkson N. Potter, 1995)

About the authors

Pippa Cuthbert is a New Zealander living and working in London. Ever since childhood, she has been passionate about food and cooking. After studying Nutrition and Food Science at Otago University in New Zealand and working in the test kitchen of Nestlé New Zealand, she decided to travel the world in search of new and exciting culinary adventures. Now based in London, Pippa works as a food writer and stylist on books and magazines, and is also involved in advertising and commercials.

From her first ice cream cone at the tender age of two, Canadian-born **Lindsay Cameron Wilson** has been passionate about food. Writing is her other passion, so she blended the two at university, where she studied History, Journalism, and the Culinary Arts. She has since worked in the test kitchens of *Canadian Living Magazine* in Toronto and *Sunset Magazine* in San Francisco. In 2001, she left her job as a food columnist in Halifax, Nova Scotia, and moved to London. That's when she met Pippa, and the work for their first book, *JUICE!,* began. Fueled by juice, the two moved on to *Ice Cream!* Lindsay continues to work as a food journalist in Canada, where she now lives with her husband, James, and baby, Luke.

Index